LIBRARY OF LATIN AMERICAN
HISTORY AND CULTURE

GENERAL EDITOR:
DR. A. CURTIS WILGUS

THE ESTABLISHMENT OF SPANISH
RULE IN AMERICA

THE ESTABLISHMENT

OF

SPANISH RULE IN AMERICA

AN INTRODUCTION TO THE HISTORY AND POLITICS
OF SPANISH AMERICA

BY

BERNARD MOSES, Ph. D.

Professor in the Unversity of California. Author of
" Democracy and Social Growth in America."

———

COOPER SQUARE PUBLISHERS, INC.
NEW YORK
1965

Published 1965 by
Cooper Square Publishers, Inc.
59 Fourth Avenue, New York, N. Y. 10003

Library of Congress Catalog Card Number: 65-21909

Printed in the United States of America

PREFACE

THIS book has been written to present the main events connected with the establishment of Spanish rule in America, and to describe briefly the more important features of Spain's colonial organization and policy. It is not designed to embrace the history of the Spanish colonies, or to furnish a rigid analysis of their constitutional law. It aims, by the use of certain historical facts, to make clear to ordinary readers and to students in high schools and colleges the origin and character of the political and economic institutions constructed for the government of Spanish America. It aims, moreover, to suggest that American history is not all told in the history of the United States, and, by making accessible in a concise form a general account of the Spanish colonies in their earlier decades, to offer an introduction to the neglected half of American history.

Parts of the volume have already appeared

iii

in print, and they are here reproduced with extensive modifications. The third chapter, " The Casa de Contratacion," was first published in the *Papers of the American Historical Association;* the fourth chapter, " The Audiencia and Viceroy Illustrated by Mexican Affairs," appeared in the *Yale Review;* a part of the eleventh chapter, " Spain's Economic Policy in America," was printed in the *University Chronicle;* and some paragraphs of the last chapter are from an essay in the *Papers of the California Historical Society.*

Spanish rule in America had its beginning in the days of Spain's enterprise and daring, and has ended in the days of her weakness and degeneracy. It embraces three general subjects for historical and political inquiry: the establishment of Spanish authority; the movement towards civilization under this authority; and the struggles of the colonies to be free. The first of these subjects is the theme of this volume.

August, 1898.

CONTENTS

CHRONOLOGICAL SUMMARY

531 : Spanish-Gothic monarchy becomes elective.
711 : Invasion of the Moors.
755 : Abderraman independent of the Calif of Damascus.
1492 : Discovery of America by Columbus.
    Fall of Granada.
1493 : Bull of Demarcation by Alexander VI.
    Columbus sails on his second voyage.
1494 : Treaty of Tordesillas.
1498 : Columbus sails on his third voyage.
1499 : Vespucius's first undisputed voyage.
1500 : Brazilian coast first visited.
1503 : India House organized.
1504 : Cortes comes to the New World.
    Columbus leaves the New World forever.
    Queen Isabella of Spain dies.
1508 : Cuba found to be an island.
    Solis on the coast of South America.
1509 : Francisco Pizarro reaches Darien.
1511 : Diego Velasquez settles Cuba.
1512 : Sebastian Cabot enters Spanish service.
1513 : Ponce de Leon discovers and names Florida.

Balboa discovers the Pacific.

1516 : Las Casas made " Universal Protector of
the Indians."
Solis in Rio de la Plata.
Ferdinand of Spain dies.

1517 : Balboa executed.

1519 : Cortes reaches the Mexican coast.
Panama founded.
Vera Cruz founded.

1520 : Magellan enters the Pacific *via* the Straits.

1521 : City of Mexico captured.

1522 : Andagoya's expedition south from Darien.

1523 : Cortes sends Alvarado to Guatemala.

1524 : Pizarro sails from Panama.

1525 : Discovery of Cape Horn.

1526 : Pizarro's second expedition.
Sebastian Cabot reaches Rio de la Plata.

1527 : Cortes's exploring fleet on the Pacific.
Audiencia for Mexico created.

1528 : Pizarro goes to Spain.
Cortes in Spain, made Marquis del Valle de
Oajaca.

1530 : Pizarro returns to America.
Cortes reaches Vera Cruz in July.

1531 : Pizarro again sails from Panama.

1532 : Cartagena founded.
Pizarro advances from Tumbez.

1533 : First printing in Mexico.
Pizarro enters Cuzco.
Atalhualpa executed.

1534 : Pedro de Alvarado reaches Peru.

1535 : Pizarro founds Lima.

Mendoza, Spain's first viceroy, in America.
First settlement at Buenos Aires by Pedro
de Mendoza.

1536 : Almagro invades Chile.
1537 : Quesada conquers New Granada.
1538 : Hernando Pizarro defeats Almagro.
Asuncion founded.
1539 : Federmann at Bogotá.
1540 : Valdivia marches to Chile.
Cabaça de Voca in the La Plata region.
1541 : Santiago de Chile founded.
Francisco Pizarro assassinated.
1542 : The " New Laws " cause civil war in Peru.
1544 : Valparaiso founded.
" New Laws " proclaimed in Mexico.
Gonzalo Pizarro enters Lima.
1545 : " New Laws " suspended.
1546 : Pedro de la Gasca reaches Panama.
1547 : Archbishopric of Mexico created.
Cortes dies.
1548 : Gasca receives the submission of Gonzalo
Pizarro ; enters Cuzco.
1550 : Valdivia killed by Araucanians.
Royal audiencia in Peru.
1551 : Ant. de Mendoza viceroy of Peru.
1552 : Las Casas prints his *Tracts*.
1554 : Alvarado enters Cuzco : defeated by Giron.
1557 : Hurtado de Mendoza in Chile.
1563 : Quinoga governor of Chile.
1564 : Spain permanently occupies the Philippines
1565 : Audiencia in Chile.
1567 : Jesuits reach Peru.

1571 : Inquisition established in Mexico.
        Tupac Amaru's revolt.
1572 : Drake on the Spanish Main.
1573 : The first Auto da Fé at Lima.
1574 : The first Auto da Fé in Mexico.
1576 : Carácas becomes the capital of Venezuela.
1578 : Drake in the Pacific.
1583 : Sotomayor governor of Chile.
1585 : Drake plunders the Spanish Main.
1590 : Hurtado de Mendoza viceroy of Peru.
1601 : Porto Bello attacked by Parker.
1606 : Archbishop Toribio dies in Peru.
1718 : India House transferred to Cadiz.
        Venezuela transferred from audiencia of
           San Domingo to audiencia of Santa Fé.
1728 : San Sebastian opened to trade with
        America.
1739 : Viceroyalty of New Granada finally estab-
        lished.
1765 : Other Spanish ports opened to American
        trade.
1767 : Expulsion of Jesuits.
1776 : Viceroyalty of Buenos Aires established.
1778 : New commercial code adopted.
1810 : Beginning of war for independence.
1824 : End of war for independence.[1]

[1] See an elaborate "Chronological Conspectus of American History" in Winsor's *Narrative and Critical History of America*, viii., 511–556.

THE ESTABLISHMENT OF SPANISH RULE IN AMERICA

CHAPTER I

INTRODUCTORY

THE popular migration through which America was settled may be contrasted with the invasion of Roman territory by the Germanic tribes. A point of difference between the two movements is seen in the fact that the Germanic tribes carried the liberalizing spirit of unconventional barbarism into regions which had developed strong social institutions, while the Europeans who invaded America went from a fully formed social organization to develop new institutions in the wilderness. In the one case, the forms of an old civilization were imposed upon the invaders, and the barbarians became hedged about by

the restraining influences of a mature social life.
In the other case, civilized society sent its
representatives to an unoccupied region, where
their essentially similar conditions tended to
produce the spirit of equality and a disregard
of the conventionalities of a complex social
existence. The members of the Germanic
tribes entered into a social organization which
had been created by the Romans. The European settlers in America had to create new
organizations adapted to new conditions. In
the one case, new life was infused into ancient
forms; in the other case, ancient forms yielded
to the modifying influences of a new life.

Spain had a large part in both of these movements. The beginning of the modern Spanish
nation is with the settlement of the invading
Germans. At the height of her power and
prestige, Spain contributed largely to the early
phases of the migration from Europe to America. The Germanic invaders of the Peninsula
took possession of a large part of the country,
introduced a new spirit, and laid the foundations of a new social life. Supplanting the
Romans, they became the dominant factor in
the early history of modern Spanish civilization. As conquerors, they took possession of
two thirds of the property in land, and by this
their supremacy was assured.

In the political results of the Germanic invasion, we observe striking evidence of the solidity of the Roman political organization. Although the Goths had broken the authority of the Romans, and had come into the Spanish Peninsula as a hostile people, yet, when they set about the work of political construction, they found nothing better to do than to take the institutions of the Empire as their model. The monarchy which they set up was " absolute in appearance, although in reality given over to the excesses of the oligarchy, by the struggles of the royal election." [1] Although the form of the rule was like that of the absolute Empire, yet in the election of the king there was revealed the Germanic spirit, the sense of independence, and the desire on the part of the people to have some share in shaping their own destiny.

Before the Spanish-Gothic monarchy became elective in 531, the headship of the tribe passed usually by the law of heredity. After this, the practice of election corresponded essentially with that carried out in the early Germanic kingdoms of England and Scandinavia. In Spain the elections degenerated, in the course of time, into struggles between a few oligarchical leaders, sometimes the representatives of families from which former kings had been chosen.

[1] Santamaria de Paredes, *Derecho Publico*, 452.

According to the *Fuero Juzgo*,[1] the power to elect belonged to an assembly composed of " bishops and of mayors of the palace and of the people." The candidates had to be of Gothic stock, and of sound morals. In the list of those who might not be elected were mentioned foreigners, those who had taken holy orders, those who were descended from a servile origin, those who had been marked with infamy, and those who had been involved in conspiracies. The conspicuous centre of the Gothic kingdom of Spain was the city of Toledo, and the elections were held, according to law, either here or at the place where the previous king had died. But the requirements of the law do not describe the historical facts

[1] The *Fuero Juzgo* was the Visigothic code or the body of laws established in Spain by the Gothic kings. " It possessed legal authority not only during the rule of the Goths, but continued authoritative even after the invasion of the Saracens, as well among the Spaniards who remained subject to the Mohammedan yoke, as among those who succeeded in maintaining their liberty in the Pyrenees or in the mountains of Asturias."

The term *fuero* as applied to the basis of municipal government signifies a charter issued by the king or by a magnate in virtue of a privilege proceeding from the sovereign, in which are contained constitutions, ordinances, and laws, civil and criminal, intended firmly to establish towns and cities, to raise them to municipalities, and to assure to them a temperate and just government, suited to the public constitution of the kingdom and to the circumstances of the towns. See Escriche *Diccionario de Legislacion y Jurisprudencia*, 728, 731.

concerning the manner and place of electing the kings; for the disturbed condition of society made it impossible in all cases to realize the provisions of the law. Royal power was often obtained by successful leadership in a rebellion, or by the fact that the candidate had been associated in the government with the previous ruler.

The period of Spanish history extending from the invasion of the Moors, in 711, to the fall of Granada, in 1492, was marked by the conflict of two unlike civilizations. The first twenty years witnessed the conquest of the Peninsula by the Mohammedans; the last seven hundred and sixty years witnessed the reconquest by the Christians. Under the Moors, the Christians were allowed to govern themselves, in minor matters, by their own laws, and their ancient magistrates exercised civil and criminal jurisdiction, but they might not impose the death penalty without the approval of the Mohammedan authorities. The Catholic worship was continued under the domination of the Moors, and was found established in the churches of Toledo and Seville when these cities were reconquered by the Christians.

During the early decades of Moorish rule in Spain, from 711 to 755, the country was under the immediate authority of a governor-general,

called an Emir, who resided at Cordova, and
was subordinated to the Calif of Damascus.
The most illustrious of the Emirs was Abderraman, who undertook to subjugate the region
north of the Pyrenees, and was overthrown by
Charles Martel. The distance of the Emir
from his superior made it impossible to maintain throughout the Peninsula a recognition of
the Calif's or the Emir's power, and to prevent
the movement towards the growth of independent local authorities. "The government of
the Emirs had reached a most unfortunate condition; the chiefs of the tribes were declaring
themselves in open rebellion; the troops were
giving themselves over to all kinds of excesses;
and anarchy began to endanger Arabian dominion on the soil of Spain." [1] In view of this
drift in affairs, it became necessary to establish
an independent power in the Peninsula, which
might check the tendency to anarchy. There
was then created the Calif of Cordova, an act
involving a revolution which set aside the
supremacy of the Calif of Damascus, established
a sovereign government in Mohammedan
Spain, and placed on the throne Abderraman, the only surviving member of the dethroned Ommeyad dynasty. Abderraman
divided his dominions into six provinces: Toledo, Merida, Zaragoza, Granada, Valencia,

[1] Santamaria de Paredes, *Derecho Politico*, 470.

and Murcia. One of the consequences of this
division was the development of the authority
of the provincial governments and the decline
of the political power of the Califs, till at last
the Calif represented merely the religious supremacy. Internal discord and hostility among
the governors weakened the Mohammedans,
and facilitated the conquests of the increasing
Christian powers.

The government of the Moors in Spain was
an absolute monarchy, in which both religious
and political supremacy were united in the
Calif. In the transfer of his power to a successor, the principle of heredity and the appointing will of the Calif were both recognized. He
might designate which of his sons he wished to
succeed him. He might associate with himself
in the government the person designated, and
cause him to be recognized as the heir to the
throne by the chief officers of the state. The
exercise of this freedom of choice was, however, often the source of dissatisfaction, and
led to social disturbance and rebellion. The
practice of dividing the political inheritance
among several sons, which prevailed in certain
contemporary Christian states, was not permitted in the Mohammedan state. The Mohammedan ruler was regarded as the bearer of
the sacred inheritance of the Prophet, which
had to be preserved and passed on undivided.

Some of the most important features of
Spanish life and policy have been determined
by the fact that Spain was for several centuries
the meeting-place of Eastern and Western culture. The Arabs and the Jews represented the
East, and the various invading tribes of Germanic Christians stood for the culture of the
West. This colliding of two great waves of
migration had a physical effect by mingling the
blood of several peoples, and a spiritual effect
in developing a peculiar quality of mind, and
in giving the nation a point of view quite its
own. When the Christians and the Mohammedans first came into conflict in Spain, both
parties were eager for the fray. The Mohammedans were rendered uncompromising by a
hundred and fifty years of unparalleled success,
and the Christians had already whetted their
zeal on the unfortunate Jews. When the
Christian rule of Spain receded before the
rising power of the Mohammedans, the con-
temned Jew, remembering the indignities he
had suffered, threw the weight of his marvellous ability and the propelling force of a holy
indignation to the side of the Moors. Under
the Moors, the Jews found their circumstances
especially favorable. They rose to positions
of honor and power. They turned again to
agriculture and the pastoral life. They took
part in the intellectual revival of the Moors;

and through the combined influence of the Moors and the Jews, Spain for a time led the civilization of Europe. The Jews not only enjoyed liberty, but they also acquired great wealth; and this wealth caused a further mixture of races. The impoverished Christians married the rich Jewesses in the hope of repairing broken fortunes; and the Jews consented to these marriages, hoping to extend their period of toleration under the Christians. And their hopes, though not on account of intermarriage, were in a large measure realized. During a part of the period of reconquest, while it was still uncertain whether the cross or the crescent would triumph, the position of the Jews in the kingdoms of Christian Spain was even higher than it had been under the Mohammedan power; and many of the characteristics of the modern Spaniard date from this period, when the blood of the Goth and that of the Jew were freely mingled.

The final victory of the Christians over the Moors meant little more than the overthrow of Mohammedan rule. Those who went with the exiled leaders to Africa, after the fall of Granada, were few compared with those who, only a short time before, had acknowledged allegiance to the Moorish government. The bulk of the subjects of the dethroned prince, Boábdil, remained within the borders of Spain, became closely allied to the other elements of the nation, and exerted a modifying influence not only on its physical qualities, but also on its intellectual tone.

The period during which Spanish territory was divided between the Christians and the Mohammedans appears, from the standpoint of social enlightenment, the most hopeful in the history of the Peninsula. The process of race affiliation and assimilation had begun, and, through the mingling of the elements present, there was forming a new nation, big with the prospects of great material achievements and of splendid cultivation. The governments of the several Christian kingdoms within the Spanish Peninsula rested on a broad basis of constitutionalism; and the local governments of the municipalities became specially conspicuous for their administration under charters of privileges, which have been justly celebrated throughout the civilized world. Looking back from our point of advantage, Spain appears in that period destined to become the successful rival of England in leading the political development of Europe. Its resources for establishing a high grade of civilization appear to have exceeded those of any other Western nation at that time.

But we have only to compare modern with mediæval Spain, in order to see that at some

point there came a change in the mental attitude of the nation, giving to its later civilization
a character which is not the legitimate outcome
of its early condition. In the early years of
Mohammedan dominion in Spain, the chief
accusation raised against the Moors was not
the familiar later charge that they were infidels;
rather that they had invaded the fields, taken
possession of the towns, overthrown the government, and in its stead set up the rule of the
usurping stranger. Towards the close of the
eleventh century, in France, Germany, and
Italy, under the war-cry of the crusades, great
undisciplined armies were moved with a holy
frenzy to throw themselves upon the infidels
of Palestine. While the fiery zeal of the crusaders was slowly burning itself out in the East,
the infection had taken in Spain, and princes
and nobles undertook a new crusade. The
ancient prospects of toleration disappeared,
and the hopes of the Jews were blasted. After
the enjoyment of power and wealth, the favor
of princes, and assurances of continued prosperity, they were compelled to abandon the land
which had become their second fatherland,
and to go into exile. These events appear to
indicate a change in the national spirit, a
turning-point in the course of Spanish civilization. The hopeful prospects of constitutionalism and municipal liberty were destroyed.

Religious intolerance and royal absolutism gave character to public action. In the sixteenth and seventeenth centuries, all European states drifted into absolute monarchy; but in some nations, as in England and Sweden, this movement was met by a resisting force in the body of the people, which rendered practical absolutism short-lived. But in Spain the transition was thorough, and the hope of freedom found no general public expression till the popular uprising in 1812.

The absolutism of the Spanish kings differed from that developed in other European states, by reason of the peculiar circumstances of Spain. In England, France, Denmark, Sweden, and the German kingdoms, the positive movement towards absolutism came after the Protestant Revolution had weakened the authority of the church in relation to the affairs of the state. But in Spain the movement fell within the years marked by the crusade against the Jews and the Moors, when the king and priests were directed by one common overpowering motive, when the royal activity was not determined by economic and political considerations, but by the desire to realize in Spain the designs of the church, involving the consolidation of ecclesiastical power and the unity of faith. The Spanish kings became, therefore, rather the champions of ecclesiasticism than the de-

fenders of the temporal interests of the nation.
To this change of attitude may be traced the
general character of later Spanish civilization,
and also many of the ills which overtook Spain
in the subsequent course of her decline. The
Jews were expelled, and thereby the nation
suffered an irreparable loss of commercial and
financial ability, that peculiar ability which
since the expulsion has been wanting in the
Spanish people, whether in Spain or America.
In obedience to the demands of awakened
fanaticism, the dominion of the Moors was
destroyed, and the beautiful cultivation of Andalusia was wasted by the conquerors. What
might have been the later condition of Southern
Spain, had it been allowed to rest under the
dominion of the Moors, it is impossible now to
determine. It is easy to say that the civilization which was destroyed had already culminated, and that it had no future but a miserable
decline into the semi-barbarism of the Orient.
It is possible that this would have been the
outcome, but the evidence presented by the
history of the Moors in Spain does not force
upon us this conclusion. Even while the
northern border of their dominions was being
pushed' towards the south by the Christians,
they continued to advance in cultivation and
the arts of peace; and in many departments of
civilized life they had never reached a higher

position than that which they occupied at the
time of their final defeat. What might have
followed their continued presence in the Peninsula, the historian may not positively affirm.
He knows, however, that whenever a nation is
observed to be advancing in a knowledge of
the arts of civilized life and in cultivation, and
still shows no decline in material resources, the
probability of a further advance, unless overwhelmed by war, amounts almost to a certainty; on this basis he infers that the upward
course of the Moors had not been fully run.

The later expulsion of the Moriscoes, in
1610, by which " about a million of the most
industrious inhabitants of Spain were hunted
out like wild beasts," had a far-reaching effect
on the material interests of the Peninsula.

" The cultivation of rice, cotton, and sugar, and
the manufacture of silk and paper had been almost
exclusively in the hands of the Moriscoes. By
their expulsion, all this was destroyed at a blow,
and most of it was destroyed forever. For, the
Spanish Christians considered such pursuits be-
neath their dignity. In their judgment, war and
religion were the only two avocations worthy of
being followed. To fight for the king, or to enter
the church, was honorable ; but everything else
was mean and sordid. When, therefore, the Moriscoes were thrust out of Spain, there was no one to
fill their place ; arts and manufactures either degenerated, or were entirely lost, and immense regions

of arable land were left uncultivated. Some of the richest parts of Valencia and Granada were so neglected, that means were wanting to feed even the scanty population which remained there. Whole districts were suddenly deserted, and down to the present day have never been repeopled." [1]

The long wars involved in these centuries which led up to the overthrow of the Mohammedans merged the interests of the church in the interests of the crown, and often made it impossible afterwards to discriminate between the ecclesiastical and political functions, between the government and the church. These wars also kept alive the fanatical zeal of the nation, and gave an ecclesiastical coloring to all great public undertakings. In this view it appears significant that the discovery of America was contemporaneous with the fall of Granada. The discovery of a new world occupied by a non-Christian people, at a time when the heroic efforts to suppress the Moorish infidel had been crowned with success, appeared to the Spaniards as evidence that they were the instruments preferred by Providence in extending the kingdom of heaven on earth. It was natural, therefore, that the exploration and occupation of America should assume somewhat of the character of a crusade. If the conduct of some of the leaders of Spanish exploration and conquest in America does not

[1] Buckle, *Civilization in England*, ii., 52.

seem to exemplify the gospel of peace and
gentleness, it should be remembered, in the
first place, that, by reason of the great distance
and the lack of communication, there were
many opportunities for the agents to depart
from the intentions of their principal, the king,
and, in the second place, that the crusaders,
whether in Palestine or in Spain, were not always averse to cruelty and even the shedding
of blood.   But the cruelty and excesses of
which the Indians of America were the victims
cannot be justly charged to the Spanish court,
but rather to the unprincipled adventurers to
whom, in a number of cases, was confided the
task of conquering and settling America.   For,
removed from the immediate control of the
court, they could and did violate its orders
with impunity.   They disregarded the commands of their superiors, and sought only their
own interests, without much regard to the
effect of their conduct on the natives.   The
accumulation of power in the crown through
the wars against the Moors had a marked influence, not only on civilization in Spain, but
also on the form and prospects of society in
Spanish America.   The policy of Spain with
reference to her American possessions was in
its essential features determined by the circumstances which made the Spanish nation and its
government what they had become.

CHAPTER II

GENERAL POLICY

THE establishment of the absolute power of
the Spanish crown made easy the adoption
of the fundamental provision of Spain's American policy, namely, that Spanish America
should be regarded and treated as directly subject to the king, and not to be controlled by the
functionaries hitherto existing for the government of Spain. When it is said that Spain
founded her rights in the New World on the
celebrated bull of Alexander VI., which was
designed to put an end to conflicting pretensions between Spain and Portugal, there is revealed an attempt to conceal the fact that the
only claims which Spain or the Spanish king
had to lands in America were based on usurpation. Carrying the pretended right back to
a grant by the pope only fixed the act of
usurpation one step earlier. But whatever
title was transmitted by the papal bull was

2

conveyed to Ferdinand and Isabella, not to the Spanish nation, and the subsequent political and ecclesiastical administration of the affairs of Spanish America was carried on under the presumption that the king was the sole political superior. From a strictly legal point of view, Mexico and Peru, and, later, the other states of equal dignity, appear as kingdoms in a personal union with the kingdom of Spain, rather than as colonies in the ordinary meaning of that term.

As a consequence of this fundamental fact of Spanish policy, the king was the most conspicuous functionary who exercised authority both in Spain and the Indies. Other political agencies were created to assist the king in administering the affairs of his American possessions, and except in very rare instances they exercised no power in Spain. They were new institutions, and were formed for the special work of governing in America. The first in rank of these special agencies was the Council of the Indies. It was created while Columbus was making preparations for his second voyage, and at the time of its establishment consisted of eight councillors. It was placed under the direction of the archdeacon of Seville, Don Juan de Fonseca. It was required to reside at court, and might be presided over by the king. It held supreme and exclusive jurisdiction in the affairs of the Indies. The separation of powers, which has become a familiar feature of modern states, was not carefully regarded in Spain in the sixteenth century. The Council of the Indies covered the whole field of governmental activity. It was a legislative body, in that from it proceeded the laws for the government of the Spanish possessions in America; it was also a judicial body, sitting as a court of final appeal for all cases concerning American affairs which were of sufficient importance to be carried to it; and it was, furthermore, an executive body, inasmuch as its advice was sought by the king on all questions of great importance in the administration of the Indies. And in order that it might be in a position to deal wisely with the affairs entrusted to it, it was a part of the king's policy to appoint many of its members from persons who had been in the public service in America or in the Philippine Islands, and had thus acquired great practical knowledge of the transatlantic countries.[1]

Provision having been made for the management of the political affairs of Spanish America by the establishment of the Council of the Indies, a second body was then created to take immediate control of the economical affairs. This body had its beginning in the exchange

---

[1] Alaman, *Historia de Mejico,* i., 35.

of Seville and the custom-house of Cadiz, which were established between the first and second voyages of Columbus.[1] When it had taken definite form, it was known as the Casa de Contratacion, which may be appropriately designated in English as the India House. It was definitely established at Seville in 1503. In this year it was ordered that a house should be built in the shipyards of Seville, for the trade and commerce of the West Indies, the Canaries, and such other islands as were already discovered, or might be discovered in the future. To this " house were to be brought all merchandize, and other things necessary to this trade," whether designed for shipment to the Indies, or to be returned from America.

This organization was made especially necessary by the plan of the Spanish king to subject the trade with America to a rigid and exclusive monopoly. Under its control, Seville became the only port from which ships might be sent to America, and through which colonial products might enter in return. The India House took account of everything that concerned the economical affairs of the Indies; it had power to grant licenses, to equip vessels, to determine their destiny, and to give them instructions as to their loading and sailing. In the performance of its ample judicial functions, it consulted

[1] Lafuente *Historia de España*, ix., 467.

lawyers, who were paid by the government. From its decisions appeal could be taken only to the Council of the Indies. Its officers consisted of a president, a treasurer, a secretary, an agent, three judges or commissioners, an attorney, and such other ministers and officials as might be provided for by law. If it is said that the Council of the Indies stood for the king in political matters, and the India House in economical affairs, the significance of the latter body is not thereby fully presented. The activity of the India House is contrasted with that of the Council of the Indies by its larger executive functions, its more immediate participation in the practical work of administration, and by acting as the agent of the Spanish king in maintaining and carrying out the laws relating to the Indies. Its jurisdiction was without special territorial limits; it covered all matters embraced in the ordinances, and reached all persons who contravened these ordinances. All cases arising from theft or any other crime committed on the voyage to, or returning from, the Indies,—in fact, all cases under the laws of the Indies—fell within its exclusive province. But in certain cases, where private persons had suffered injury on the voyage from other private persons, the injured party might demand justice either before the judges of the Casa or before an ordinary court of Seville.

In these two organizations, the Council of
the Indies and the Casa de Contratacion of
Seville, we discover the two special agents employed by the king in carrying out in America
the measures of an essentially absolute rule,
whether they concerned the political or the
economical affairs of his possessions. But
the immediate direction of Spanish-American
affairs was intrusted to single officers and councils residing in the New World. Prominent
among these were the governors, the audiencias,
the viceroys, the presidents, the captains-general, and the officers of the municipalities.
With whatever authority they were clothed,
they were all subordinate to the king and the
Council of the Indies, or the India House; and
under whatever titles they existed, they were
all designed to contribute to the two great
features of Spanish colonial policy, namely,
absolute political control and monopolistic
privilege in industry and trade.

The first step in carrying out the restrictive
commercial policy which Spain had adopted
was to limit the commerce with America to a
single Spanish port. Seville became the privileged port, and so remained for about two
hundred years, until, by the decree of 1717,
the India House, with all its privileges, was
removed to the port of Cadiz. The actual
transfer was made in 1718. Down to this

time no power had been adequate to break Seville's exclusive privilege. Whatever ships went to America were cleared by the authorities of the port of Seville, although in certain cases they may have actually set sail from the bay of Cadiz. Ten years later, in 1728, the privilege of Cadiz was invaded. The Company of Guipúzcoa was granted the privilege of trading with the province of Caracas from the port of San Sebastian. This was the only exception in the policy of exclusiveness till 1765. Then came a change through which other Spanish ports were opened to the American trade; and finally, in 1782, Spanish subjects or members of the colony of New Orleans were permitted to take cargoes from French ports, and return to these ports the wares of Louisiana and Western Florida. But, as indicating the survival of the Spanish infatuation, these traders were not permitted to enter money at the ports of France.

But the restriction as to ports was scarcely less severe at the American end of the route than in Spain. At first ships might sail to America whenever they were ready and had received the proper license; but later they were allowed to go only in fleets and under a naval escort. This was the usual order for two centuries, till 1748, and while it prevailed two fleets were sent annually, one to Porto Bello,

on the Isthmus, the other to Vera Cruz, in
Mexico. Although controlled immediately by
the India House, the fleet might not be announced, nor the officers chosen, except under
the order of the Council of the Indies.

Under this arrangement, all trade with Mexico had to pass between the port of Seville and
that of Vera Cruz; and all trade with South
America, between Seville and Porto Bello, trade
between the several colonies being strictly prohibited. Panama thus became the port of collection and distribution on the Pacific. The
exports from the Pacific coast of South America
were gathered here and carried across the
Isthmus to Porto Bello, and here was held a
fair of forty days' duration, at which the European wares were exchanged for the gold and
silver and other products of America. For
decades the intercourse between Spain and
Spanish South America was annually confined
to the few days of unloading and loading the
ships of the Spanish fleet. The fair of Porto
Bello was, therefore, the great event of the
year for the whole of South America. From
it European wares were distributed to Venezuela, Granada, Peru, Chile, and even to Buenos
Aires. But by this system of transportation
the prices of the imported wares, at certain
places, were increased by five hundred or six
hundred per cent. of the original cost. This

fair was more especially the great event for the little town of Porto Bello. On the arrival of the vessels, most of the inhabitants of the town were accustomed to quit their houses for the advantage of letting them, while others retired to a few rooms in order to make money out of the rest. The poorer quarters were naturally overcrowded, and barracks were erected, principally for the accommodation of the ships' crews, who here kept stalls for the sale of sweetmeats and other things brought from Spain. " But at the conclusion of the fair, the ships put to sea, all these buildings were taken down, and the town returns to its former tranquillity and emptiness." [1]

The prices of the wares which were exchanged at the fair of Porto Bello appear to have been determined by comparing the wares brought from Spain with the silver, gold, and other articles from Peru, and setting the one amount against the other, having no regard to any consideration except that of relative amounts. [2]

[1] Ulloa, *Voyage to South America*, i., 90.

[2] Concerning trade between Spain and her American colonies, see Rubalcava, *Tratado Historico, Politico, y Legal de el Comercio de las Indias Occidentales*. Of the variations of prices at the Isthmus, Benzoni says that at Nombre de Dios, where Spanish ships were accustomed to land various articles, the prices at different times varied greatly, on account of the uncertainty and irregularity of the supply. The principal articles received there were wine, flour, and biscuit. Besides

The usefulness of the fair at Porto Bello became known to the merchants of New Spain, and they requested that a similar fair should be established in that kingdom.   This plan was not carried out till the beginning of the eighteenth century.   It was then determined that the fair should be held in Jalapa, to which place the wares landed at Vera Cruz were transported by land.   The decree establishing this fair was issued April 12, 1728.   But before this time the effectiveness of the commercial system had already begun to decline under the encroachments of contraband trade.[1]

these there were cloth, silk, oil, and other things for household use, made in Spain.   "And sometimes it has happened, that the market has been so overstocked, that the articles did not fetch the price which they originally cost in Spain.   I have even seen some instances of people having various goods left on their hands, such as oil, figs, raisins, *et cetera*, and not being able to obtain any price for them, they have left them with the captain of the ship for freight.   Whilst, on the contrary, there have been times when everything was so scarce, in consequence of the ships not coming (owing to fear of the French), that every article was sold, as the saying is, for its weight in gold."—*History of the New World*, 116.

[1] Rubalcava, 181.

CHAPTER III

THE CASA DE CONTRATACION

WHEN the India House was organized to manage the trade with America, it was proposed that a building should be constructed for the use of the officers; but by a subsequent order of the same year, 1503, this plan was set aside, and the offices which had been created were kept in the old Alcazar. The clerk, whose business it was not only to keep and report the accounts, but also to secure and preserve the books, papers, and records of the trade, was later known as the contador, or accountant. It was at first intended that the commissioners should live in the India House. In 1518, however, Charles V. ordered that no one should live in the House, but that it should be held exclusively for trade and the meetings of the officers. In order that the officers of the House might issue proper directions, they were ordered to " consult with, and receive information from,

27

such persons as were acquainted with the countries discovered "; and the judges of other courts were ordered not to encroach upon their jurisdiction.

The formation of a special corporation at the port of Seville, through which should pass the affairs of the Indies, was one of the first practical indications that these affairs were to be regarded as belonging particularly to the crown and not to the civil authorities of Spain. In view of the opposition which this policy aroused, the king ordered the " supreme magistrates of Seville not to intermeddle, on any account, with what concerned the jurisdiction of the India House, but rather to diligently support and maintain it in the privileges granted by him." [1] Similar commands were issued subsequently, and they were accompanied with the statement that he would not only maintain the new institution, but would add to its authority if necessary. Under Philip II., its authority was, in fact, extended so that it was a repository not only for the treasures brought from the Indies, but also for certain revenues raised in Andalusia. Even the fitting out of the great Armada of 1588

[1] Veitia Linage, 7. The references given here are to *Norte de la Contratacion de las Indias Occidentales*, by Don Joseph de Veitia Linage, "made English" by Capt. John Stevens under the title *Spanish Rule of Trade to the West Indies*.

was entrusted to the president and commissioners of the India House, acting in conjunction with the Duke of Medina Sidonia. Their power increased; their credit rose; they appointed officers of fleets and civil magistrates; they granted passes to ships; and in importance and dignity they stood next to the royal councillors. They enjoyed the same privileges and immunities as the judges of chancery and of the other courts. They exercised civil and criminal jurisdiction in all cases involving the owners and masters of ships, sailors, factors, and merchants, and those intercepting letters or instructions relating to the Indies. They took cognizance of all crimes committed while sailing to, or returning from, the Indies, and in these cases no other judges had power to intermeddle; and, according to a decree of 1558, the same method of procedure was followed as in the royal courts of Valladolid and Granada.

Persons violating the ordinances of the India House might be brought from any part of the Spanish king's dominions, and be tried by this body in its judicial capacity in Seville. As a court it had, moreover, full jurisdiction over its own officers. In 1655, one of the accountants killed another in a street in Seville, and a contest between the India House and the city as to the jurisdiction in this case was decided in favor of the former of the contestants. Not

only had the India House the extensive jurisdiction here indicated, but it was also subordinate to no council but that of the Indies.
And it had power to inflict any degree of
punishment.

In accordance with the provisions of the
ordinances, the president, " appointed to reside and preside in the India House," was
required to be a " person of note and experience," " well versed in the affairs of the Indies," having knowledge of places, of the
history, and of the voyage. He bore the title
of Lordship, and, in 1628, an order of the
council of war decreed that the president was
so careful of his dignity that he never acted
jointly with the regent of Seville on any public
occasion, because of difficulties of precedence,
and in making visits of compliment he was attended by two judges or commissioners, and
the *alguaciles* were accustomed to go before the
coach.   All the elaborate ceremonies attending
his taking up the duties of his office were carefully prescribed by law.[1]

Among the duties of the president, one of
the most important was the fitting out of the
fleets and the armadas. He was, moreover,
expected to supervise the embarkation of passengers, taking special care that none should
go without a license, and that licenses should

[1] Veitia Linage, 19, 20.

not be sold or counterfeited. The general
ordinance prohibiting the officers of the India
House from engaging, either directly or in-
directly, in the trade with America, applied to
the president as well as to all other officers.
The punishment of any president found guilty
of violating this ordinance was reserved to the
hands of the king.

After the president, the most important
officers were the judges, who enjoyed the distinction of being styled *jueces officiales*, a title
which all other officers belonging to the West
Indies were forbidden to assume. For a number of years they had the power to appoint the
high officers of the fleets, but after the creation
of the Council of the Indies this power fell
into the hands of that body. Yet the admirals
and vice-admirals continued subordinate to the
judges of the India House; they enjoyed
supreme authority only when under sail; " and
as soon as in their return they cast anchor in
any port of Spain their authority ceases, and
is transferred to the judge, or commissioner,
who goes down to receive or clear the ships." [1]

The law not only determined the order of
business, but also prescribed the office hours
of the members. They were required to be on
duty three hours in the forenoon of each day,
from seven to ten, during the season from

[1] Veitia Linage, 26.

Easter to the end of September, and from
eight to eleven during the rest of the year.
And if any one were absent without just cause
it was provided that his salary for that day
should be withheld.   The rule fixing the hours
of the judges was not always observed, for
" when there are Armadas or Flotas to fit out,
or clear, they sit at all hours and times, without excepting the greatest holiday, or unseason-
able times at night; so that as no hours are
exempt from business, upon extraordinary oc-
casions, so that when there is no business they
do not sit in the afternoon." [1]

No judge, or commissioner, was permitted
to be absent without leave.   At first, while
there were only three judges, leave was granted
by the king, and the absent judge was obliged
to secure a deputy; but later, after the number
of officers had been increased, it became customary for the president to grant such leaves
of absence as were not for more than thirty
days. [2]

The members of the India House were
divided into two bodies, called the chamber
of direction or government, and the chamber of
justice.   For eighty years, or until the founding of the chamber of justice, in 1583, the whole
business of the institution was conducted by a

---

[1] Veitia Linage, 27.   [2] *Ibid.*, 28.

single body. During the first fifty-four years of this period, this body was composed of three judges; and during the last twenty-six years, of three judges and a president. After the creation of the chamber of justice, this body took cognizance of all criminal cases; but cases not involving the king's revenue, nor specified in the laws and ordinances of this court, might be tried before this or any other court, at the pleasure of the parties concerned.

The chamber of justice, as established in 1583, consisted of two lawyers who were called judges, but were distinguished from the *jueces officiales*, or judges by office. A few years later, in 1596, a third judge was added, in order to avoid a tie, and to permit all cases brought before the chamber to be decided. All matters of law and justice were determined by the judges who were lawyers. If a case were originally brought up in the chamber of direction, and there were developed in the course of its consideration contests belonging to a court of justice, it was immediately turned over to the chamber of justice. In this court suits were terminated with a hearing or a re-hearing, but cases involving more than 600,000 maravedis, or 1500 dollars, might be appealed to the Council of the Indies. All cases involving the revenue, or duty for convoys, or pay due from the king, or sums in charge of the House,

3

which might not be delivered by an order of a
court of justice alone, could not be taken up by
the chamber of justice until after they had
been presented to the chamber of direction.
If it were disputed whether an item of business
belonged to the chamber of direction or to the
chamber of justice, the point in question was
referred to the president and one judge from
each chamber. For all matters not covered
by the particular laws of the India House,
resort was had to the general laws of the kingdom.

Besides the officers already mentioned, there
was a fiscal, or solicitor, who has been described as '' the king's mouth in causes wherein
he is concerned, a check upon those that manage the revenues, a spy upon those who em-
bezzle it, an informer against those that defraud
it, an agent to improve it, and lastly a two-
edged sword in a civil and criminal capacity,
to defend the patrimony of the crown.'' This
office was first established in 1546. Before
this time, one of the commissioners had been
appointed to perform its duties. He was required to keep a record of all suits managed
by him for the king, and to pass it on to his
successor. His duties, in fact, were those of
a prosecuting attorney, but his action was
limited to cases concerning the king or his
revenue; and his cases took precedence of all

others. One of the duties of the commissioners was to go to the port and dispatch the
armadas or fleets, and also to receive them on
their return. This was regarded as one of
their most unpleasant duties, and was performed in turn, beginning with the eldest. An
extra allowance for this service of six ducats a
day was made to each commissioner performing it, and twelve ducats a day to the president.
This duty consisted in inspecting the ships,
determining whether or not they were in a
proper condition to be sent to sea. If repairs
were needed, the extent of them was determined, and they were ordered to be made. If
they were overloaded, a portion of the freight
was ordered to be removed; and great care was
taken that no goods should be put on the vessels after they had been cleared. To prevent
this, no boats except those properly licensed
were permitted to go over the bar with the
fleet. The commissioners clearing the vessels
were required to send the officers of the king
at the ports to which the ships were bound, an
account of the destination of the ships, what
force of men and guns they carried, what
freight, and the extent of their provisions. It
was the duty of the commissioners, moreover,
to prevent the shipment of passengers without
the proper licenses from the king or council.
In case passengers were shipped without such

licenses, a penalty of one thousand ducats was imposed upon the officer under whose command they were carried. The commissioner dispatching vessels was required, moreover, to see that the ships carried a sufficient amount of provisions and fresh water, and that they were ready to sail at the proper time. Having set sail, all the merchant ships were required to follow the admiral, to approach and salute him every day, and not change their course without his leave, '' on pain of death and forfeiture of goods.'' [1]

There was a general prohibition that no magistrate or officer of justice in the kingdom of Spain should interfere in any matter falling within the jurisdiction of the India House; and that no seaport officers should go on board vessels bound to, or returning from, the Indies. In going from Seville to Cadiz to dispatch vessels, the commissioner took with him one of the clerks and a constable. He made the journey on the barge belonging to the India House, or on a vessel hired for him for this purpose.

On the return of ships from the Indies, they were received by some judge or commissioner of the Casa. This duty, like the duty of dispatching vessels, devolved in turn upon the several members of the organization. The

[1] Veitia Linage, 45

smaller ships were received in Seville near the Golden Tower. Those that were unable to ascend to this point on the river were received at a place called Barego, while those that came in fleets were always received in the port of Bonança.[1] In 1589, it was ordered that no one but a judge, or commissioner, from the chamber of direction of the India House should be given a commission to visit the armadas or flotas. The thorough inspection involved in the commissioner's visit appeared to be necessary in carrying out Spain's protective policy. It involved mustering the men to see if those who had left Spain had returned; also an examination to determine whether the vessels carried the guns and ammunition which under the law they were required to carry, and to find out if they had observed their instructions as to landings, or had brought goods not properly entered. The commissioner was also required to determine "whether there was any blasphemous person aboard, or any that kept a wench; or whether they had played at prohibited games, or committed any other crimes."[2] If, on inquiry, the commissioner found that the master owed the sailors any part of their pay, he was required to command that the payment be made within three

---

[1] Veitia Linage, 47.   [2] *Ibid.*, 48.

days; and if this command was not obeyed, the master was arrested and ordered to pay an additional sum to each person to whom he was indebted for every day of delay in making payment. If it appeared, from the oath taken by the master and the crew, that any person had died on the outward or return voyage, an account and an immediate delivery of his goods were demanded; and if the goods were not immediately delivered, the master was required to pay the amount of their value, and forfeit to the king double this amount. In his official inspection, the commissioner was required to find out whether any slaves or passengers had been admitted on board the vessels without leave, and whether any Indians had been brought from America. This last had been strictly prohibited under penalty of a large pecuniary fine, perpetual banishment from the West Indies, and a payment for the return of the Indians to the province or island from which they had been taken. If the person guilty of this offence was unable to meet the payment for the return transportation, he was condemned to suffer a hundred lashes. In case persons belonging to the ships were absent at the time of the inspection, it was at first the practice to have them brought before the president and the court, but later they were brought before the commissioner at the port. The re-

sult of this leniency was that often a majority
of the men were absent from the muster, and
this led to the imposition of a small fine for
leaving the ship before the inspection. Not
only the merchant ships but also the men-of-
war were inspected on their arrival, with the
view of determining whether they had com-
plied with the prescriptions of the law.

It was incumbent on the India House to
render to the Council of the Indies the earliest
possible information concerning the arrival of
the galleons and flotas. In pursuit of this purpose, the commissioner at the port, on the first
intimation of the approach of vessels, sent out
a boat to bring this information, which he at
once dispatched by an express to the India
House, however imperfect it might be.

As soon as the vessels had reached the port,
a second messenger was dispatched to carry to
the India House the number of the ships and
a statement of the treasure which they contained. This information having been received
by the president, was by him immediately sent
to the king. The process of unloading the
vessels was indicated in the law with great de-
tail. The chests, with letters and accounts,
were conveyed to Seville by a special messenger as rapidly as possible.

" The plate is unloaded out of the ships into

great vessels called *gavarras*, or lighters, that of
each galleon apart, an *escrivano* certifying the bars,
chests, or other parcels so unloaded, upon which
every boat has its guide, and a waiter appointed to
bring it up. This is when the ships unload in the
port of Bonança, for if it be done in Cadiz, an officer with some soldiers is to be in every boat, the
whole cargo being in charge of the admiral's captain, who goes in one of the said boats, and the
ensign or sergeant in each of the others, with such
number of soldiers as the admiral shall appoint."[1]

In the first phase of its organization the India
House comprised three judges or commissioners. As judges they had some functions in
common, but in addition to these each had
certain peculiar administrative duties. One
commissioner was at the same time the comptroller. He kept a detailed account of all sums
received by the treasurer, and of all bills drawn
upon these sums. He was required to preserve
the " entries of ships sailing to, or returning
from, the West Indies, upon pain of paying
the damage the party shall sustain whose entry
is lost."[2] For the management of the affairs
of his office he was permitted to have a certain
number of subordinate officers and clerks. The
most important of these was a deputy comptroller, who took charge of all matters belonging to the king's revenue. In case the

[1] Veitia Linage, 52.　　　　　[2] *Ibid.*, 56.

comptroller was sick or absent, the deputy was empowered to sign for him and to dispatch all the business of the office. In appointing deputies to any commissioner, great care was taken to exclude all such persons as were in any way concerned in trade in the West Indies.

Among other officers subordinate to the comptroller, there was one who took charge of the goods of deceased persons, the goods of persons absent, and property left in trust. This officer, whenever the occasion arose through illness or absence, might act for the deputy comptroller. Another officer was charged with making the entries of commodities passing through the India House. There was still another officer whose duty it was to have a book in which was kept a record of persons departing for the Indies, their names, places of birth, and the names of their parents. Another officer or clerk had charge of the credits and the uncoined silver. He also conducted the correspondence between the court on the one hand, and the king and private persons on the other. All these officers held commissions approved of by the chamber of direction. Such other clerks might be employed in the comptroller's office as were demanded by the business in hand.

Some idea of the details of this office may be had from a list of books kept in the regular course of business. They were as follows: 1. Books of receipts and expenditure, in which were entered

"all the charges, in a very plain and distinct method, mentioning what chest the sum came from, what hands it has gone through, whether it came entire, in what sort of coin, and if it be ingots of gold or silver, in what shapes, upon what terms it was sold, mentioning the particular number of bars or other pieces of gold or silver, with the numbers, fineness, and weight, and whether they weighed the same as they did in the Indies." [1]

In these books were entered also orders for payments, and these orders were the comptroller's receipts for his disbursements. 2. Books of the revenue derived by the *cruzada*.[2] 3. Books of the king's private revenue. These contained accounts of the sale of gold and silver ingots, which were sold at the treasury. These accounts embraced statements of the number

[1] Veitia Linage, 58.

[2] Every two years the bull of the *cruzada* was published containing " an absolution from past offenses by the pope, and, among other immunities, a permission to eat several kinds of prohibited food during Lent, and on meagre days. . . . Every person in the Spanish colonies, of European, Creolian, or mixed race, purchases a bull, which is deemed essential to his salvation, at the rate set upon it by government." The price varied, according to the rank of the purchaser, from two reales to sixteen reales. See Robertson, New York, 1839, 1, 384, 523.

and weight of bars, the persons to whom they
were sold, and the dates and terms of sale.
4. Books wherein were entered all the commodities deposited in the warehouses. 5. Books
in which were recorded all the resolutions of
the chamber of direction. 6. Books of the
dead, in which a record was kept of all property
that belonged to deceased persons, " stating
accounts nicely with the dead, making him
creditor for all that is brought over in armadas
and flotas, and debtor for all that is delivered
to his heirs, executors, and creditors."[1]   7.
Books in which were entered the fines and
the expenses of the court. 8. Books of passengers, in which were entered the names,
birthplace, and parentage of all persons going
to the Indies the places of their destination,
and the terms of their licenses.   9. Books
of letters, embracing copies of all letters written by the court.   10. Books in which were
filed copies of all orders, bills, informations,
and certificates.   11. Books in which were entered or filed the commissions of all the officers
of the India House.   12. Books in which were
filed copies of all naturalization papers that had
been issued to persons to enable them to participate in the trade with the West Indies.   13.
Books in which were charged all utensils and
goods delivered to the chief pilot, cosmog-

[1] Veitia Linage, 59.

rapher, and other officers.   14. Books in which
were kept accounts of the loading of all ships.

Another commissioner held the special office
of treasurer, and whatever money was received
from the sale of gold, silver, pearls, and other
products of the Indies was committed to his
custody. The treasurer and the other commissioners were required to give bonds to the
amount of thirty thousand ducats, each, and
the treasurer, as the receiver of the money of
deceased persons, an additional bond of fifteen
thousand ducats, while of the sub-treasurer
there was required a bond of ten thousand
ducats. The treasury chamber to which the
laws make frequent reference was a room with
barred windows and double doors.   Each door
had three unlike keys which were distributed
among the commissioners.

Payments of money belonging to the crown
were made on orders issued by the king,

" passed by the councils of the West Indies and
of the Revenue, in such manner that the Council
of the Indies gives an order for the gross sum; and
then that of the Revenue grants particular warrants
to those who are to receive it.   These warrants are
presented in the chamber of direction, where as-
signments are given upon the treasurer." [1]

The sums belonging to deceased persons,

[1] Veitia Linage, 62.

which came into the hands of the treasurer
were very great during the early decades of
Spanish dominion in America, and it became
customary to make loans from this store. In
1633 the king had borrowed from it more than
five hundred thousand ducats, and all the
pressure that could be brought to bear upon
him was inadequate to make him restore it.
It, therefore, happened that persons holding
valid claims against this fund could not recover
what was due them, because the fund itself
had been exhausted by loans to persons who,
like the king, either could not or would not
meet their obligations. In order to avoid com-
plications and embarrassments from delayed
claims, steps were taken to ensure that the
most efficient means possible should be taken
to discover the heirs in all cases; but in case
they did not appear or were not discovered
within two years after inquiry for them had
been instituted, the property of such deceased
persons should be regarded as forfeited. The
property of deceased persons here intended included not only that of persons who had died
in the Indies, but also that which had been left
by passengers, sailors, and others, who had
died on the outward or return voyage. For
managing this property the treasurer, by a decree of 1671, was granted a fee of one per cent.
of all that came into his hands.

The third of the three judges, or commissioners, who at first constituted this court of
trade, held in addition to his office of commissioner, the special office of factor, or manager.
His principal function was to purchase on behalf of the king, or the king's officers, commodities needed for the king's service in
America. If a governor, or any other officer,
of the king's appointment in the Indies, had
need of any material from Spain for the proper
conduct of affairs in his department of public
service, he sent to the factor at Seville or
Cadiz, who purchased the desired articles and
sent them to him by the ordinary means of
communication. The factor, moreover, was
charged with all commodities brought from
the Indies for the king, or brought by the
king's order to be sent thither, except gold,
silver, and precious stones. These were consigned to the treasurer. Using the king's
arsenal as a storehouse for the things received,
the factor was accustomed to deliver them on
an order from the king, the council, or the
chamber of direction. The actual care of
the commodities was confided to a deputy of
the factor, who occupied an apartment in the
building in which they were kept. Although
the king's gold and silver were in the custody
of the treasurer, yet if any of it was to be
melted down at the mint, the supervision of

this work devolved upon the factor. And he had, moreover, the control of the funds advanced by the king for carrying the ecclesiastics to the Indies, and furnishing them those things which they might need, and to which they were entitled under the law.

One of the important articles of trade between Spain and the Indies was quicksilver, which was extensively used in the production of silver. The trade in this particular commodity was monopolized by the king, and no other person might engage in it, under penalty of death and forfeiture of property. It having been found that the mine of Almaden did not produce enough to supply the demand of New Spain, it was determined to make up the deficiency from the mines of Peru. For three or four years, therefore, quicksilver was carried from Peru to New Spain, and, as a part of this transaction, goods of various kinds were carried from New Spain to Peru, thus violating the law prohibiting trade between these two countries. Although this trade may have been mutually advantageous to the two colonial kingdoms immediately concerned, it was nevertheless regarded by the king as detrimental to the interests of Spain, and was consequently suppressed. The subsequent failure of the Peruvian mines caused the Indies for a certain time to be supplied entirely from Europe, principally from

Germany and the mine of Almaden. Whatever part was sent from Spain passed through
Seville, and was prepared for shipment under
the care of the factor or manager of the India
House. The manner of putting it up has been
described by Veitia Linage, sometime treasurer
and commissioner of the India House:

" Every half-quintal, or half-hundred, is put into
a sheep's skin well bound with hempen cords, and
that into a tight cask, nailed down, and three of
these casks containing a quintal, or a hundred
and a half, into a chest, which, being nailed and
bound over with hempen ropes, is wrapped with
coarse mats, and bound over again. Upon every
chest is fastened the king's arms painted on linen
cloth, and these chests are for New Spain; for
those carry but a quintal that are for the Firm-
land." [1]

To avoid the danger of the skins rotting, it
was found advisable not to form the packages
until the ships were ready to sail.

" A commissary was appointed to go in the ships
that carry quicksilver, who gave bonds to the factor
for the delivery of them to the king's officers at the
port they were destined for, and to make good the
deficiencies of the regular convoy duty the masters
were obliged to pay for such goods as they take
aboard. These commissaries were appointed by

[1] *The Spanish Rule of Trade to the West Indies*, 68.

the president of the India House, and being brought before the chamber of direction, gave security; and for their trouble and hazard were allowed twelve ducats for every eighteen quintals, accounted a ton, which was paid by the king's officers, where they delivered the silver." [1]

For one hundred and twenty-two years the organization known as the India House consisted of three commissioners who, as already indicated, filled the several offices of comptroller, factor, and treasurer. In 1625, Philip IV. added the Duke of Olivares to the list of commissioners, at the same time conferring upon him the office of chief *alguacil*, which was made hereditary to the immediate heirs of his family. The list of judges or commissioners was also increased by the creation of the office of chief *alcalde*, or keeper, which was conferred upon the Count of Castrillo, and made hereditary to his heirs forever. It devolved upon him, among his other functions, to appoint the doorkeepers of both the chamber of justice and the chamber of direction, and their assistants, the doorkeepers of the office for convoy money, the porter at the gate, the keepers of the treasury chamber, and certain other officers of the custom-house and port, all of whom had previously been appointed by the president of the Council of the Indies.

[1] *The Spanish Rule of Trade to the West Indies*, 69.

4

The historical significance of the organization known as the Casa de Contratacion lay in the fact that for a long time it held the key to the New World, and was the efficient agent of the Spanish king in carrying out the most rigid system of commercial restriction that was ever framed.   It continued to have its seat at Seville till 1717, when it was transferred to Cadiz for greater convenience in superintending the shipping to America, the bulk of which at this time went from, and was received at, this port. After the removal to Cadiz, an agent of the India House continued to reside in Seville, as, while the offices were in Seville, there had been an agent in Cadiz.   The actual transfer of the offices to Cadiz, in accordance with the decree of 1717, was made, as already indicated, in 1718.[1]

The attitude of Spain towards trade and traders was such as to furnish a positive hindrance to commercial development; and in the course of time the Spaniards had to lament that, through their failure to honor and encourage merchants, most of their trade had fallen into the hands of foreigners.   In view of the tendency towards this result, certain special privileges were extended to Spanish merchants trading with the Indies.   Among these privi-

[1] Antunez, *Legislacion y Gobierno del Comercio de los Españoles con sus Colonias en las Indias Occidentales,* 10.

leges may be noted that of deferring payments
to creditors in case of misfortune causing considerable loss. Any person who had been
granted this privilege through letters of license,
was accustomed to pay five per cent. per
annum on the amounts of the payments de-
ferred.

It was one of the rules of transportation that
goods must be landed at the port to which they
were consigned; and if they were permitted to
be sent to adjacent ports, it was required that
they should be sent thither in other vessels
than those which carried them from Spain.
Goods brought from the Indies consigned to
the king were always introduced into Spain free
of duty. Provisions and other commodities
sent for the use of the soldiers in the garrison
in Florida also paid no duty. After import
duties had been removed, it was customary to
allow goods for use in Spain to be taken from
the ships wherever they might come to anchor,
but goods imported for re-exportation had to
be brought to Seville that arrangements might
there be made for the duty of exportation.
In the later times the duties were so exorbitant
that the officers did not pretend to collect the
full amount. It appeared from experience
that by this means the maximum revenue
would accrue to the state, because of the extraordinary efforts that were made to escape

payment altogether when the full duty was demanded.

Important among the burdens imposed upon the commodities involved in the trade between Spain and the Indies was the *haberia*, or duty levied on the goods carried, in order to meet the expenses of the convoy. It was first imposed in 1543, and was then at the rate of two and one half per cent., and in 1587 it was raised to seven per cent. After the sea had become somewhat more safe by the cessation of hostilities between England and Spain, the rate of convoy fell to six per cent., but it appears to have risen again in the first half of the seventeenth century; for by a decree of Philip IV., dated 1644, it was ordered that this duty should not exceed twelve per cent. All commodities whatsoever carried to, or brought from, the Indies, not excepting those belonging to the king himself, were required to pay this duty. No goods were delivered until the duty for convoy had been paid, and this was exacted, although the goods had on another account been forfeited. Yet silver and commodities consigned for the holy places at Jerusalem and for the redemption of captives were exempt from this duty. The collecting and accounting for this duty was at one time entrusted to the commissioners of the India House; but after 1572 it was placed in the hands of a special commission of five persons, who sat in a chamber of the India House, which had been appointed for their use.

Besides the functionaries already mentioned, there was also a *proveedor*, or commissary-general, whose duty it was " to order all payments for provisions bought," and to see that no more provisions and stores were taken on board than were needed for use. This officer was subordinate to the president and commissioners of the India House, and all agreements which he might make required their approval in order to be valid. He was permitted to employ four agents, or under-commissaries, and was required to render an account of all provisions turned over by him to the officers of the ships taking charge of them. Such provisions were free from all duties. The *proveedor* might appoint a deputy to act in his absence, and also two clerks, when the amount of the business demanded it.

Among the other persons employed in connection with the shipping to America, mention may be made of the superintendent of the workmen engaged in the shipyards. He was expected to examine the ships needing repairs, and to oversee the work of repairing, preventing waste through dishonest work or the stealing of material. The master carpenters and master calkers were appointed by the king, on

the recommendation of the commissioners of
the India House. They were paid by the day
whenever they had work. There was also a
storekeeper who had charge of all provisions
and material for fitting out ships, and who
delivered them as they were needed, " from
the time the ships began to be fitted till they
sailed." During part of the colonial period
there were two of these officers, and at other
times three.

The visitors of ships were important officers of the India House. They have been
described as next to the commissioners in
dignity. They were required to be " expert
and skilful " in fitting out ships, to inspect
them, and to determine the number of men
and the amount of stores and ammunition
that should be put on board of each. Before
leaving for the Indies each ship was required
to have a license from the president and commissioners of the India House, and to have
been examined either by the president and
commissioners themselves or by the visitor.
The ship was examined before it was loaded,
in order that it might be seen if it were sea-
worthy in all respects and well ballasted. In
addition to these precautions, it was provided,
in 1609, that no ship under two hundred tons
burthen should be admitted to the convoyed
fleet. It was customary to have every ship

visited three times. "The first visit was for
the visitor to appoint how the vessel was to be
fitted; the second, to see whether all had been
performed that had been ordered; and the
third, to clear it for sailing." [1] The third visit
was that already referred to as made by the
president or one of the commissioners of the
India House. He was accompanied by a
visitor, who was to see that the ships were not
overloaded, that no freight was carried on
deck, that a sufficient amount of provisions
had been taken on board, that the vessels carried the requisite amount of arms and no more,
and that they had on board no unlicensed passengers or wares not properly entered. At the
sailing of a vessel, the business of the visitor
with reference to it was ended, for on the return of the ships the visitor had nothing to
do with them. [2] In addition to these officers,
there was a large number of clerks and other
subordinates, who had in hand the mass of
details relating to the trade between Spain and
America.

Concerning emigration to the West Indies,
it was provided, in 1511, that any subject of
Spain, on properly entering his name, might
be allowed to go to the Indies. But later, in
1518, in 1522, in 1530, and in 1539, orders were
passed involving restrictions, in accordance

[1] Veitia Linage, 98. [2] *Ibid.*, 99.

with which the bar of exclusion was raised
against all persons newly converted from Juda-
ism or Mohammedanism to the Catholic faith,
against the children of such persons, or the
children and grandchildren of persons who had
worn the Saint Andrew's cross of the Inquisition, and against the descendants of any person
who had been burnt or condemned for heresy.
Any person violating these provisions was liable
to forfeiture of property, a hundred lashes, and
perpetual banishment from the Indies.   To
prevent violations of the restrictive laws concerning emigration, it was provided by a royal
order of 1552,

" that for the future, the judges or commissioners
of the India House should not suffer any person
whatsoever, though of such as were allowed, or
though he had the king's letters of license, to go
over to the Indies, unless they brought certificates
from the places where they were born, to make
appear whether they were married, or single, de-
scribing their persons, setting down their age, and
declaring that they were neither Jews nor Moors,
nor children of such, nor persons newly reconciled,
nor sons or grandsons of any that have been punished, condemned, or burnt as heretics, or for
heretical crimes; such certificates to be signed by
the magistrates of the city, town, or place where
such persons were born." [1]

[1] Veitia Linage, 108.

A few years later, in 1559, the prelates in the Indies were instructed " to inquire whether there were any Jews, Moors, or heretics in those parts, and to punish them severely." And in 1566, all the sons and grandsons of heretics were excluded from offices or places of trust.

All magistrates, captains, pilots, masters, mates, or other persons, aiding in the violation of these restrictions on emigration were subject to a great variety of penalties, fines, lashes, banishment, imprisonment, and transportation to Spain, which were increased to such an extent that in the beginning of the seventeenth century it was decreed that passengers who should go to the Indies without the proper leave, " should be sent to the galleys for four years, or, if they were persons of quality, to Oran for ten years." This penalty should also be imposed on masters of ships, and in addition a fine of one thousand silver ducats. In 1607, it was provided that any sea officer carrying passengers to the Indies without leave should be punished with death. But in the course of time the extreme rigor of the law was abated in favor of a pecuniary fine. Yet the severer measures continued to have supporters, since the removal of restrictions caused the countries to be overrun with peddlers, who cut off more or less of the trade of the established merchants.

The president and commissioners of the
India House, without reference to the king,
might grant leave to go to the Indies, to
mestizos, who had been brought to Spain; to
merchants, even such as were married, provided
they had permission from their wives, and left
a thousand ducats as a guarantee that they
would return within three years; to agents of
merchants in the Indies, but only for three
years; and to inhabitants of the Indies, who
were known to have wives there. Any other
person required a license from the king.

When the question arose as to what persons
should be regarded as merchants, the title was
interpreted so as to include any one who had
shipped goods rated for the payment of duties
at seven hundred and fifty dollars or more.
Married women whose husbands were living in
the Indies might go to them and be accompanied by a kinsman within the fourth degree
of consanguinity; but if the husband went to
Spain for his wife he was not permitted to return without a license from the king. And the
privilege of going to the Indies was strictly
withheld from all single women.

Although the president and commissioners
of the India House might permit merchants to
go to the Indies without their wives for a
period of three years, provided they had the
wives' consent, and left the guarantee of one

thousand ducats, yet no other married man, not even a governor or other officer of state, was allowed to go without his wife, except under an express dispensation from the king. And without this dispensation, the wife of the highest officer as well as the wife of the ordinary man was required to bring the same proofs of identity that were required of the men.

How rigid was the restriction imposed on emigration may be seen from the fact that although one held a commission for employment in the Indies, and even a pass from the king, he was not permitted to sail without a license from the India House. It was not, however, to be expected that all persons would bring their certificates of qualification in the exact form required by the law; and when there were deficiencies in the papers presented, such deficiencies were sometimes supplied by information gathered by the officers of the India House; and sometimes in order to avoid the great inconvenience that might be caused by delay, a pass or license was issued on the receipt of satisfactory security that certificates in due form would be subsequently forwarded from the proper sources.

The rules governing the passengers on the voyage required that they should carry their own provisions, and the masters of ships were prohibited from undertaking to furnish them food. The passengers were, moreover, required to swear that they would not remain at any port at which they might stop on the way to their proper destination, and that they would not carry their goods ashore before they had been examined. If one carried a license to reside at a specified town in the Indies, he was expected to reside there; and if one pretended to be going to the Indies to exercise a certain handicraft, he was obliged to follow it.[1] And there were rules prohibiting persons from going from one province to another without leavē from the king. Similar restrictions were imposed upon persons going from the Indies to Spain. They might not leave without permission " from the viceroys, presidents, or governors of the places of their habitation." And the governors of seaports were prohibited from granting leave to any person residing in their jurisdiction, except on the presentation of a license from the civil officer within whose jurisdiction he lived.

By an ordinance of 1560, it was provided that persons going to the Indies without license should forfeit to the crown all property acquired there, with the exception of one fifth part which should go to the informer; and they should, moreover, be arrested and sent as prisoners to Spain at their own expense. Neither they nor

[1] Veitia Linage, 113.

their heirs might receive goods sent to them;
and in accordance with a bull issued by Alexander VI., they were declared to be excom-
municated.

If the royal ordinances which touch on
the ecclesiastical affairs of America indicate
the will of the Spanish kings in this matter, the
kings were moved by a strong desire to promote the religious welfare of the Indians. Pre-
supposing this desire, the restrictions which
were placed on the emigration of friars and
priests appear as means for preventing any but
those of virtuous and exemplary lives from
going to the Indies. These restrictions were
carried out through orders to the commissioners of the India House not to allow the
friars of any order to go without a license.
Persons attempting to avoid this provision
were seized and sent back to Spain. As early
as 1530, an order was issued to the commissioners of the India House, requiring them not
to permit foreign friars to go to the Indies,
even if they had leave from their superiors.
This prohibition was confirmed by later ordinances, under which it was required that all
applications by ecclesiastics for passes should
be referred to the Council of the Indies. In
1664 the privilege of entering upon missionary
work in the Indies was granted to Jesuits under
certain restrictions. The members of the re-

ligious orders who went to America under these
conditions went at the king's expense; but
they were obliged to restore to him the amount
of his outlay in case they returned to Spain
without leave. In the course of time, by reason of the rise of prices, the allowance which
had been granted in the beginning for these
expenses was found to be quite inadequate,
and whatever further amount was needed by
the friars was made up by the orders to which
they belonged.

Friars of the orders of Carmelites who went
shod were specially prohibited from going to
the Indies, but this prohibition did not stand
against the barefooted friars of this order.
After the beginning of the seventeenth century, the prohibition was made to apply to all
orders which had not already established monasteries in America. By an act of the council
it was provided, in 1665, that no friar having
returned from America to Spain would be
allowed to go back, even though he had a
license, unless, on his arrival in Spain, he had
reported to the council the cause of his return.
The long list of ordinances limiting the movements and general activity of the members of
the religious orders indicates to what marvellous lengths and into what minute details
Spain's restrictive system extended.

In keeping with the restrictive policy of **the**

Spaniards, all foreigners were forbidden to trade with the Indies, without a special license from the king; and, having obtained such license, they were limited to dealing in their own wares, and might not, even if naturalized, become owners or masters of ships. By foreigners were meant all persons not born in the kingdoms of Castile, Leon, or Aragon. Later the territory, to be born in which constituted one a native in the meaning of the law, was extended so as to include Navarre, Valencia, and Catalonia. The class of persons known in Spain as natives was further extended by the decree of 1562, and made to embrace such foreigners as had been settled householders in Spain for ten years, and had married a Spanish or an Indian woman. But residence, even for more than ten years, did not confer this privilege on bachelors. In 1608 the line was drawn more strictly. Twenty years of residence, including ten as a householder, were required; also marriage with a native or with a daughter of a foreigner born under Spanish dominion.

In order to avoid the effect of these provisions, foreigners who were

" not capacitated to trade, contrary to the known laws, sold their commodities to subjects and natives of these kingdoms, to be paid for them in the Indies, by which means the gold and plate, brought from those parts, was carried to other countries, and that very often, before it came into Spain." [1]

This practice led to the passage of special ordinances prohibiting it. These were confirmed at different times, and death and forfeiture of goods fixed as penalties for their violation. An attempt was, moreover, made to prevent foreigners from trading in the Indies by ordering that persons residing there should not purchase commodities of foreigners, on pain of forfeiting half their property and of being returned to Spain as prisoners. By a later law, foreigners were forbidden to reside in the Indies, and those already there were expelled; yet in the course of time the harshness of this law of expulsion was toned down by lax execution. In spite of the severe measures taken against foreigners attempting to trade with the Indies, or to reside there, it was decreed that foreigners residing in Seville and at adjacent ports, although they might not engage in the India trade, should nevertheless be obliged to contribute to the fitting out of armadas and fleets, and to all other expenses borne by the Spaniards.

The intimate relation between the king and his American dominions necessitated a regular organized system of postal communication.

[1] Veitia Linage, 127.

As early as 1514, by a royal warrant, Dr.
Galindez de Carvajal was made postmaster of
the Indies, and by a subsequent order of the
Council of the Indies, issued in 1524, all persons were restrained from interfering with him
in the dispatch of messages concerning the
affairs of the Indies. The lines of this service
covered the distance between Seville and the
other ports, and Madrid, as well as the distances
between Spain and America. The postmaster
of the Indies was an officer of the India House.
His duties were " to receive all dispatches sent
by the president, commissioners, or other officers, or by the prior and consuls, and other
persons trading to the Indies." He provided
means for sending messages to the court and
to the various ports, by keeping post-horses at
certain stations. The service was rendered by
persons appointed by the postmaster, who were
prohibited from making any charges above the
rates fixed by law. The customary speed at
which messages were transmitted under this
system was thirty leagues a day. Rigorous
laws enjoined all persons from intercepting and
opening letters and packets. Of the amount
paid for this service the postmaster was allowed
one tenth part.

The laws and ordinances contain abundant
details concerning the organization and control
of the royal navy and fleets of merchant ships

5

engaged in furthering the India trade. The admiral, or captain-general, held the chief command, and while on the sea was clothed with power which was essentially absolute; yet he was under oath " that he would not avoid death in defense of the faith, of his master's honor and right, and of the public good of the kingdom." The admirals and vice-admirals, before beginning to exercise the functions of their offices, were obliged to present their commissions and instructions to the officers of the India House, and to furnish the required security that they would faithfully perform the duties of their offices, or meet whatsoever fines might be imposed upon them. The amount of the security demanded varied according to the dignity of the office, ranging from three hundred ducats, in the case of the physician, to five thousand ducats, in the case of the admiral.

After having crossed the bar of San Lucar, the admiral's vessel took the lead, the other vessels followed, the ship of the vice-admiral held her position in the rear, and the other men-of-war kept to the windward of the merchant vessels. If any ship strayed from the fleet, a fine was imposed upon certain of her officers, and they were excluded for a series of years from making this voyage; but if a ship was wilfully taken from the fleet, the guilty officers suffered death and forfeiture of prop-

erty. After putting to sea, the admiral or
vice-admiral examined all the ships. If goods
were found that had not been properly entered
they were confiscated; and if passengers were
found without a license they were set on shore
at the Canaries and sent back to the prison of
the India House.

CHAPTER IV

THE AUDIENCIA AND VICEROY ILLUSTRATED
BY MEXICAN AFFAIRS

DURING the process of exploration and
settlement, authority in America rested
in the hands of leaders of expeditions and
colonies, who usually bore the title of *adelantado*.[1] This was the title formerly applied in
Spain to the military and political governor of
a frontier province. Standing face to face with
the Moors, he held the general military command of the province, and had power to gather
the people under his standard. In his capacity
as a civil officer, he took cognizance of such
civil and criminal cases as arose within the
limits of his territory.[2] When Spain found

[1] Santamaria de Paredes, in *Derecho Político*, p. 487, has
described the *adelantados* as "governors of great territories,
with a character chiefly military." The military officers under
the *adelantado* were *maestro de campo*, *sargent mayor*, and
alferez real ; see Makenna, *Historia de Santiago*, i., 37.

[2] Escriche, 89.

herself extending her Christian dominion over regions that had been held by the American infidels, it was natural for her to apply to the leaders in this undertaking the title which the champions of Christian Spain had borne during the long contest with the Mohammedans. This title was borne by Columbus and by most, if not all, of those who founded colonies in districts not hitherto occupied by Spanish authority.

In the course of colonial growth, the *adelantado* was superseded by a collegiate power known as the *audiencia*. In Spain, this body was a superior tribunal of one or more provinces, composed of officers learned in the law, who represented the king in the administration of justice.[1] But in America the audiencia wielded governmental power in all departments. To it were confided in the beginning, and later in the absence of the viceroy, all matters with which governmental authority might properly deal. It was held to be the principal care of the Supreme Council of the Indies to give the Indians spiritual and temporal instruction, yet on account of the inconvenience of distance this charge was committed to the audiencias.[2] The audiencia exercised not only judicial and political functions, but in the absence of any superior officer it was also the

[1] Escriche, 304.   [2] *Politica Indiana*, 395.

chief authority in military affairs. In judicial matters, even in the presence of the viceroy as president, the audiencia exercised a large measure of independence. In such cases the viceroy had no vote, and the administration of justice was left to the judges, or ordinary members of the audiencia. The viceroy, however, signed the decisions with the judges, in accordance with the practice of the presidents of the audiencias of Spain.[1]

The most important audiencias in America were those of San Domingo, Mexico, Guadalajara, Guatemala, Panama, Santa Fé de Bogotá, San Francisco del Quito, Lima, La Plata, Caracas, Buenos Aires, and Santiago de Chile. In 1555 the jurisdiction of the audiencia of Lima extended over the whole of South America; but later several audiencias were established within the limits of the authority of the viceroy of Peru; as in New Spain the audiencias of Guatemala, Mexico, and Guadalajara were under the general dominion of the viceroy of Mexico. The Philippine Islands were governed for a time by a special audiencia, but about 1590 they were made dependent on the

[1] *Recopilacion de Leyes de Indias*, lib. ii., tit. xv., Ley 32. Robertson, vol. i., 352, says: "The viceroys have been prohibited, in the most explicit terms, by repeated laws, from interfering in the judicial proceedings of the courts of audience, or from delivering an opinion, or giving a voice, with respect to any point litigated before them."

viceroy and audiencia of Mexico, and were immediately subject to a governor. In accordance with a royal decree of 1593, New Spain was the only part of Spanish America that might send vessels to, or receive goods from, these islands. Yet the connection between these two regions subject to a common authority was not intimate; the voyage from Acapulco and the return lasted thirteen or fourteen months, and one vessel a year sufficed for this trade.

The great power of the audiencia in judicial matters may be seen in the fact that there was no appeal from its decisions, except in civil suits of more than ten thousand *pesos de oro*, in which there was an appeal to the king.[1] It was the highest judicial authority in America. It appears to have been formed on the model of the ancient supreme court of Spain; at the same time it was for its special district what the Council of the Indies was for the whole of Spanish America. Matters of grace, appointments to office, and *encomiendas* belonged to the governors or viceroys as presidents of the audiencias. In case of a grievance arising on account of a decision of the viceroy or president in matters of government, an appeal might be taken to the audiencia, in accordance with the laws and ordinances, and the viceroys and presidents could not prevent such an ap-

[1] Markham, *History of Peru*, 120.

peal.[1] That in some respects the powers of the
viceroy and the audiencia were co-ordinate may
be seen in the fact that each without informing
the other might correspond directly with the
king. When there were several audiencias
within the limits of the viceroy's jurisdiction,
the presidents and judges of the subordinate
audiencias were required to keep the viceroy
informed of the affairs of their several districts; and these subordinate audiencias were
required to take account of, and carry out,
the decrees concerning military and political
affairs which the viceroys might send to them.[2]

In the language of a specific law, " the
president and judges of the royal audiencia
of Guadalajara, in New Galicia, shall obey
the viceroy in everything, and hold with him
the good relation which is befitting one who
represents the king."[3] In case the position
of viceroy or governor was vacant, the audiencia, whose president was thus wanting, might
grant Indians in *encomienda ;* and it was specially provided that while the office of viceroy
of Peru was vacant, the audiencia of Lima
should assume the control of governmental
affairs not only in Peru but also in Charcas,
Quito, and Tierra Firme, exercising all those

---

[1] *Recop.*, ii., tit. xv., Ley 35.
[2] *Ibid.*, Ley 49.
[3] *Ibid.*, Ley 52.

powers which under other conditions belonged
to the viceroy; and during this time the audiencias of Charcas, Quito, and Tierra Firme
were required to obey and subordinate themselves to the audiencia of Lima. This order
of things belonged, of course, to the period
before the establishment of the viceroy of New
Granada. Similar powers devolved upon the
audiencia of Mexico, whenever the post of viceroy became vacant. The president and judges
of the audiencia of Guadalajara were required to
recognize and obey the superior authority of the
viceroy of Mexico, and the same attitude of subordination was required of the governors of
Yucatan and New Biscay, and of other royal officials within the limits of the jurisdiction of the
viceroy of Mexico. Whenever, on account of the
absence of the viceroy, the audiencia assumed
the direction of governmental affairs, the oldest
judge was made president, and empowered to
perform all the functions belonging to that
office. Among the powers of the president of
the audiencia was embraced that of appointing
judges to fill irregular vacancies.

In their judicial capacity the audiencias of
Lima and Mexico were not employed as courts
of first instance, but under certain conditions
they might hear both civil and criminal cases.
Decisions rendered by the audiencias were determined by the vote of the majority, and they

were then signed by all the judges, although
some of them might have held dissenting opinions. In addition to its judicial and executive
functions, the audiencia was expected to keep
elaborate records of decrees concerning the
Indies, of judgments pronounced, and of the
movements of persons within the limits of
migration permitted by law.

The first royal audiencia regularly established
in America was that of San Domingo. For a
short time this was the chief Spanish authority
in the Indies. It was composed of a president,
who might act as governor and captain-general,
four judges, a fiscal, an alguacil mayor, a deputy
of the grand chancellor, and such other officers
as were found to be necessary. Among the
audiencias established in America, there was no
prescribed uniformity in the number of members. In the course of time the number of
members in the several audiencias was changed,
in view of the increasing population, and in
obedience to the demands for a more efficient
government. They varied also according to
the importance of the country of residence,
ranging from four members upwards. The
audiencia of Mexico was composed at one time
of four judges, at another time of ten. That
of New Galicia was composed of a regent and
four judges. The audiencia of Mexico had
three fiscals, that of New Galicia one. The

former was organized in such a way that two sections dealt with civil affairs, and another with criminal affairs. In ordinary cases the oidores, or judges, of the audiencia formed the decisions, but in cases of great import other judges were called to sit with them.

Originally all the islands of the West Indies and the neighboring portions of the mainland were under the jurisdiction of the audiencia of San Domingo. But after the establishment of the audiencia of Mexico, this latter body embraced within its jurisdiction the provinces of New Spain, Yucatan, Tabasco, Nuevo Leon, and Tamaulipas, on the Atlantic coast; on the Pacific coast it extended to the limits of the jurisdiction of the audiencia of Guatemala, on the south, while on the north it extended to the territory of New Galicia. The audiencia of New Galicia embraced within its jurisdiction the provinces of Guadalajara, or Jalisco, Zacatecas, and the region west of these provinces, together with Coahuila and Texas.[1]

The audiencia of San Domingo had been influential in extending the conquest to the continent. From San Domingo had proceeded the conquest and settlement of Cuba; and from Cuba had proceeded the expedition led by Cortes for the conquest of Mexico. Diego Velazquez was the governor of Cuba, and the

[1] Alaman, *Historia de Mejico*, i., 49.

expedition was organized under his authority, and in part at his personal expense. Cortes received his appointment from him, but very early determined to act on his own account. Velazquez suspected this determination on the part of Cortes before the expedition set sail, but too late to repair the mistake of having appointed an insubordinate leader of an expedition on which he had spent a large part of his own fortune. The breach between Cortes and Velazquez was never healed, and all the efforts of the governor to regain his lost advantage only resulted in his impoverishment and ruin. Cortes, on his side, bent his energies to getting his undertaking recognized by some other power than the governor of Cuba. Therefore soon after his landing on the coast of Mexico he caused to be organized the municipality of Vera Cruz. It was established on his initiative, and the officers were nominated by him. This was the first political organization effected by Europeans on the soil of Mexico. The two alcaldes were Puertocarrero and Montejo, the latter an adherent of Velazquez, and the former a member of the Cortes faction. In view of the limitations placed upon the expedition by the audiencia of San Domingo, Cortes's right under Spanish law to found a city is questionable. But a municipal organization was, nevertheless, formed, and, whether revolutionary in its origin or not, its powers were at least recognized by the leader of the expedition. Into the hands of this body Cortes surrendered his authority and retired; but the next morning he was informed that he had been elected captain-general and justicia-mayor of the municipality. If Cortes designed this manœuvre to place behind him for his support some other power than the governor of Cuba, it was in a measure successful, although the adherents of Velazquez denounced the whole proceeding as a conspiracy. At certain periods when warfare was the conspicuous feature of Spain's activity, the military leader of a Spanish municipality had held a position of recognized dignity and power, and it is possible that Cortes aimed at this advantage.

Before Cortes received any commission directly from Spain, he was authorized, in 1522, by the audiencia of San Domingo " to conquer the whole of New Spain, to brand slaves in accordance with prescribed rules, and to distribute *encomiendas*." Although this authorization was provisional, it nevertheless came from the supreme representative of the Spanish crown in America, and gave a character of legality to the efforts of Cortes to extend the dominions of Spain. In October, 1522, the authority which had come to him provisionally from the audiencia of San Domingo was confirmed by a

commission issued by the emperor.   This commission bestowed upon the conqueror of Mexico the titles of royal judge, governor, justice,
and captain-general, and was accompanied by
an expression of the emperor's appreciation of
the services which Cortes had hitherto rendered.

There is little doubt that Cortes fancied that,
having taken possession of Mexico, he would
be allowed to proceed according to his own
will without much interference from the Spanish crown, and that it would be possible for
him, supported by the Indians, to maintain independent authority.

" He wrote a letter to the Spanish crown, the
language of which is little known, in which, while
he insisted in the plainest manner upon his services
and personal devotion, he in the most courtly
terms denied allegiance, and declined any interference of the royal officers in the administration of
the new colony." [1]

The Spanish crown had sent four officers to
Mexico to take charge of the royal interests.
These were the treasurer, Alonso de Estrada;
the accountant and paymaster, Rodrigo de Al-
bornoz; the factor, Gonzalo de Salazar; and
the inspector, Peral Mendez Chirinos.

His conquests in Mexico completed, Cortes

[1] Bandelier, *The Gilded Man*, 115.

directed his attention to establishing means of
protection, and his fundamental idea appears
to have been originally derived from European
feudalism. Every settler possessed of *repartimientos* of less than five hundred Indians was
required to provide himself, within six months
from the date of the ordinance, with a lance, a
sword, and a dagger, a helmet, two pikes, and
either Spanish or native defensive armor.
Holders of *repartimientos* with from five hundred to one thousand Indians were required to
possess, in addition to these implements of
war, one horse fully equipped; while those
with *repartimientos* with more than one thousand Indians were required to maintain a still
larger equipment. These vassals of the govern-
or were obliged to keep themselves in readiness
to answer a summons at any time, and the
municipalities were authorized to call them
from time to time for a review, and to exact
penalties in case of their non-compliance.

The municipality of Mexico, like that of
Vera Cruz, was created through the appointment by Cortes of municipal officers, among
whom Pedro de Alvarado was given the place
of the leading alcalde. In 1522 this city had
become so conspicuous that the king was moved
to grant it a coat-of-arms. Seven years later
its pre-eminence in New Spain was officially
recognized, and in 1548 it was entitled the

" very noble, great, and very loyal city."
This method of constituting a municipality
was, however, not always followed even in
these years, for the municipal organization that
was finally removed to Oajaca was constituted
through an election by the settlers. Not long
after the municipality of Mexico was established
by Cortes, the appointing power of the govern-
or was limited, and he was required to act in
this matter jointly with two other royal officials,
and to appoint each officer from a list of three
which had been nominated by the people. The
number of regidores, or members of the town
council, was, moreover, increased from four to
six, and some of them were appointed by the
king for life.

The troubles in New Spain arising out of the
clashing interests of jealous parties and the inefficiency of the audiencia of San Domingo
in dealing with distant affairs, led to the establishment of an audiencia at Mexico. It was
deemed prudent to curtail the conqueror's
power, and it was believed that no single minister would be able to do it. There was clearly
needed, moreover, some force to put an end to
local quarrels, and to give to all persons, particularly to the Indians, the protection of an
authoritative government. On the 13th of
December, 1527, the audiencia was created by
the appointment of four oidores, or judges.

These were Francisco Maldonado, Alonso de Parada, Diego Delgadillo, and Juan Ortiz de Matienzo.[1] Although ordered to embark immediately, they did not sail from Spain until July, 1528. As was customary later, in the case of the passage of the viceroy from Spain to America, the vessels which conveyed them were placed under their command. In view of the fact that there was no suitable public building in Mexico in which they might be accommodated, the emperor requested Cortes to receive them in his palace, and gave orders that they should be obeyed throughout the conquered region. At the time of their appointment, the conduct of Cortes was under investigation before the emperor, and after some delay Nuño de Guzman, governor of Panuco, was appointed president of the audiencia, to hold office till the termination of Cortes's trial. Guzman arrived in Mexico in December, 1528.

Of the three audiencias within the later jurisdiction of the Mexican viceroy, that of Guatemala was next in importance to that which had its seat in the City of Mexico. The territory subject to its authority lay between that under the audiencia of Mexico and the northwestern limit of the lands under the government of Santa Fé de Bogotá. The conquest of this

[1] See Icazbalceta, *Don Fray Juan de Zumárraga*, 18.

6

region had been undertaken from many sides and at different times. Perhaps the most important expedition which had undertaken the exploration and settlement of the country was that under Alvarado, sent by Cortes from Mexico in 1524. Alvarado entered from the northwest, and at first made himself master of the district of Soconusco, which lies between the Pacific and the mountains, at the extreme northwestern part of the country.

The capital city was founded in July, 1524, at a point which the subsequent eruptions of the volcano rendered untenable. Alvarado, as governor and captain-general of the conquered district, appointed the officers of the municipal government. Diego de Roxas and Balthasar de Mendoza were made alcaldes; Pedro Puerto-carrero, Herman Carillo, Juan Perez Dardon, and Domingo Zubiarreta, regidores, and Gonzalo de Alvarado, chief alguacil. The first meeting was held on the 27th of July, when Diego Diaz was appointed receiver-general. The organization was known as a city from the beginning, for it was recorded by the secretary that on the 29th of July, " the alcaldes and regidores of this city of St. Iago took their seats in council." At another meeting, on the 12th of August, the office of sacristan was conferred upon Juan de Reynosa, and ninety-seven persons were registered as citizens. Thus was organized the city of Santiago de los Caballeros de Guatemala.

Alvarado remained the governor and captain-general of Guatemala till his death in 1541. During the first four years he acted under the authority of a commission from Cortes; afterwards his authority was derived directly from the emperor. Probably no other region of Spanish America presented such a confusion of titles and authorities as that which was under the general dominion of the audiencia of Guatemala. Its several parts were immediately controlled by a great variety of officers, but between their several territories and jurisdictions the boundary lines were only partially and imperfectly drawn.

Among the lower local officers, the governors held the first position. They were the heads of provinces. In each city which was the capital of a province, the government was organized under a *corregidor*. Other subdivisions of the province were called partidos, and were governed by *alcaldes mayores*.[1] These officers were magistrates, who, under the inspection of the viceroy and the tribunals, exercised police, military, and judicial functions; in a word, they found themselves charged with whatever might contribute to order and the public tranquillity. They were forbidden by law to en-

[1] Mora, i., 174.

gage in trade, yet from the beginning they violated the law openly and without hindrance.[1] Other officers of the cities were the alcaldes, regidores, and sindicos, who composed the *ayuntamientos*, or town councils. The alcaldes and the regidores, except in cases where a part of the regidores were appointed for life, were elected annually by the citizens of the town. In the course of time some of the officers of the municipality became not only entitled to hold their positions for life, but they might also transmit them to others by inheritance or sale. Every town which had an *ayuntamiento* was called a *villa*, or a *ciudad*, and the difference between these was indicated by the number of the alcaldes and regidores, less in the *villa* and greater in the *ciudad*.[2]

The unsatisfactory state of the early public administration of Mexico, under the audiencia, persuaded the king of Spain to subject the country immediately to a kingly rule, and to place a viceroy in direct control of affairs. It seemed to be necessary to make the headship of the government of such dignity that it might not be attained by an adventurer. The viceroyalty having been established, it became customary to appoint the viceroy from among the distinguished nobles of the Spanish court. They were thus supposed to be placed above

[1] Mora, i., 201.   [2] *Ibid.*, 175.

the avarice and low ambition which had marked the career of the officers of the first audiencia. But before this plan was carried out, it became necessary to send a new audiencia organized like the first; and whatever hopes were entertained of better results were based on the care taken in the selection of the members. The four oidores, or judges, nominated by the president of the audiencia of Valladolid, were Juan de Salmeron, Alonso Maldonado, Francisco Ceynos, and Vasco de Quiroga. The presidency of the new audiencia was conferred upon the bishop, Fuenleal, who at the time of his appointment was president of the audiencia of San Domingo.

The instructions of the oidores were dated July 12, 1530, and provided that in the absence of the president the senior oidor should preside; the audiencia should protect the natives; it should dispatch all unfinished business pending before the first audiencia; it should proclaim the *residencia* of the officers supplanted, sending the papers to Spain; it should restore to Cortes his estates, and maintain friendly relations with him. In case President Guzman were found not guilty by the residencia, he should return to Panuco. The members of the new audiencia took their seats on the 12th of January, 1531, but the president did not arrive from San Domingo till the following September. It was found later that the work which devolved upon the audiencia was so great, that, in order to facilitate its execution, the president appointed two additional oidores for a term of two years.

Soon after sending the second audiencia to New Spain, the emperor carried out the suggestion to make that country a viceroyalty. Antonio de Mendoza was appointed viceroy. His commission was dated at Barcelona, April 17, 1535. He was granted a salary of six thousand ducats, three thousand as viceroy, and three thousand as president of the audiencia. There was also granted the sum of two thousand ducats for the expenses of his bodyguard. In 1614, the salary of the viceroy of Mexico was fixed at twenty thousand ducats.

The viceroys, presidents, judges, and other royal officers in Spanish America were hedged about with numerous restrictions. They might not hold more than one office; they might not marry or contract for marriage within the districts of their authority; and their sons and daughters were under the same restriction. They were prohibited from engaging in any form of commercial enterprise. They might not leave their districts without a special license from the king or the Council of the Indies; and they might not hold more than four slaves apiece. In the affairs of the government, the viceroy was expected to seek the advice of the audiencia, but that body had no power to determine his decision, yet in judicial matters the oidores were supreme, and the viceroy had no vote. He might, however, exercise the functions of captain-general.

The viceroy, who in the person of Mendoza now appears for the first time in Spanish America, represented the person of the king of Spain. He stood at the head of the vice-regal government, exercised his vast governmental powers with justice equally to all his subjects and vassals, and urged such measures as conduced to their peace and elevation. On assuming his duties, his first care, as indicated by the law, was to provide for the service of God and the preaching of the Christian faith for the benefit of the natives and the inhabitants of the provinces. He was charged to govern and defend his kingdom, to reward services rendered in the exploration, pacification, and population of the Indies; to collect and remit funds due the royal treasury; and to do everything which it would devolve upon the king to do were he governing in person, except in cases of special prohibition. All other officers and subjects, ecclesiastical and secular, were ordered to respect and obey him as the representative of the king. He was president of the royal audiencia, was captain-general of the provinces within his dominions, and in the exercise of his powers maintained the state and dignity of royalty. His court was " formed upon the model of that at Madrid, with horse- and foot-guards, a household regularly estab- lished, numerous attendants, and ensigns of command, displaying such magnificence, as hardly retains the appearance of delegated authority." [1]

Even before the newly appointed viceroy had reached the Indies he was treated with distinction. On arriving at Seville, he was lodged in the Alcazar, and, accompanied by his family and guard, was transported to America without charge. On the voyage, the viceroy was general of the armada, or fleet, from the time of his departure from the port of San Lucar till his arrival at Porto Bello or Vera Cruz. In order to avoid the temptations to depart from a wise and impartial administra- tion, the viceroy was enjoined from taking with him his married sons or daughters, his sons-in-law and his daughters-in-law. He was ordered, on the outward voyage, in passing the cities of Porto Bello and Cartagena to in- spect the public works, the artillery, the muni- tions, and the men-of-war, and to send to the king a detailed account of their condition and needs. Whenever the viceroy of Mexico was

[1] Robertson, i., 351.

promoted to the viceroyalty of Peru, he was at
liberty to take with him his furniture and
wardrobe, and all his servants, slaves, and
other persons in his employment, without paying duty, but he was obliged to pay the accustomed costs of transportation. While making
the voyage from Mexico to Peru he was regarded by the generals, admirals, captains,
masters, and owners of vessels as their superior, and they were required to obey and salute
him, when not impeded by the peculiar circumstances of the voyage. When the viceroy entered the capital of Mexico or Peru for the first
time, those engaged in the industries and trade
might not be required to go out to receive him;
nor should the towns and villages through
which he passed be required to pay the expenses
of his journey.

At the beginning of his term of service the
viceroy obtained information as to the condition
of affairs in his dominions through conferences
with his predecessor, from whom also he received the papers belonging to the office. His
duties in punishing crime were not limited to
acts committed during his term of office, but
extended to crimes committed under his predecessors. He exercised also the power of
pardoning within his dominions under essentially the same condition as the king in Spain.
He kept a record of the distribution of the In-

dians, and acted as a judge of first instance in cases in which they were involved; and in these cases an appeal lay to the audiencia. He had, moreover, the power to place the Indians in positions of feudal dependence, as provided by the laws relating to *encomiendas*, in case they were not already in this position at the time he assumed the duties of his office. The viceroy of Peru might be attended by a captain and fifty soldiers, and each soldier should receive a salary of three hundred dollars, and the captain six hundred dollars. The viceroy of Mexico might be attended by a captain and twenty soldiers. The term of the viceroy's service was fixed at three years, counted from the day of his arrival in the City of Mexico or Lima; but he might hold his position for a longer or a shorter time, according to the will of the king. In Peru he received a salary of thirty thousand ducats, in Mexico twenty thousand; and these amounts were reckoned from the day on which he assumed his duties till the arrival of his successor, it being provided that there should not be paid at any time two salaries for the same post. For the journeys from and to Spain six months each were allowed, and both voyages were made at the public expense.

Mendoza arrived in Mexico in 1535. He was made president of the audiencia and acting captain-general. His authority extended to all affairs of government; but at the same time his position furnished no exception to the rule under which nearly all the offices of Spanish America were ordered, namely, that every office in the administration should be checked in the exercise of its functions by some other office. The viceroy might be checked by the audiencia, and both might correspond directly with the Council of the Indies. " But any beneficial effect which this might have had in protecting the people, was counteracted by the inordinate power of the viceroys, and their consequent means of influencing the audiencia, and every other subordinate authority, civil, military, judicial, or ecclesiastical." The viceroy's power was, however, in certain respects limited. He could not create offices and increase salaries without the especial authority of the king. He could not extend the term of an office beyond the point fixed by law; and if any person should hold office under such pretended extension, for his services during such time he should receive no pay.

On his arrival at the capital Mendoza was received with marked distinction by the public authorities; but on this first occasion of the reception of a viceroy the ceremony was much simpler than it became later. In the course of time the whole journey of the viceroy from

Vera Cruz to Mexico assumed the character of a triumphal march. Arches were erected along the way, and the inhabitants of the towns through which he passed came out in holiday attire to do him honor. His entrance to the capital was made the occasion of displaying all the magnificence which the city could lavish on a high state ceremony. The expenses attending this display became at length so great that the king issued a decree limiting to eight thousand dollars the sum that might be expended for this purpose on any single occasion.[1]

The most important political event in Mendoza's reign of fifteen years was the publication of the " New Laws." These laws proceeded from the Council of the Indies, under the sanction of the emperor, and were designed to bring about new relations between the Indians and the Spanish settlers. Under the system of *repartimientos* or *encomiendas*, the Indians had been the serfs or slaves of the Spaniards. At first, while Columbus was governor in the Indies, lands were apportioned to Spaniards, with authority to require them to be cultivated by a certain specified *cacique* and his people. Later, under Governor Ovando, of San Do-

---

[1] In *A Voyage to South America*, ii., 46–52, by Don George Juan and Don Antonio de Ulloa, the ceremonies attending the public entrance of the viceroy at Lima are described at length.

mingo, an *encomienda* of a certain number of Indians was granted, and the grant of Indians was not always accompanied by a grant of land. The *encomienda* has been defined as

" a right, conceded by royal bounty to well-deserving persons in the Indies, to receive and enjoy for themselves the tributes of the Indians who should be assigned to them, with a charge of providing for the good of those Indians in spiritual and temporal matters, and of inhabiting and defending the provinces where these *encomiendas* should be granted to them."

The clause in the terms of the grant requiring that the Indians should be taught " the things of our holy Catholic faith " was from the first treated as a mere formality, and had little or no influence in determining conduct. The change in the character of the grants, from those made under Columbus to those made under Ovando, was a change from serfdom to slavery. When pressed by suitors for royal favors, Ferdinand, having little else to give, gave Indians; and some of the recipients of these gifts intended to go to the Indies, while others intended, as absentee proprietors, to farm out their Indians.

On February 22, 1512, the king issued from Burgos an ordinance providing that no one, of whatever station, in the Indies should hold more than three hundred Indians under the laws providing for their distribution among the settlers. If any one had more than this number, the excess should be taken away and distributed among the neighboring residents; and if, at the expiration of thirty days after the publication of this ordinance in the island of Española, any one were found to have more than the prescribed number, he should be deprived of all he had, and in the future would be incapable of holding others. In such a case the person making the accusation would be entitled to one third of the Indians, and of the other two thirds, the judge rendering the decision should receive the fifth part, while the other four fifths should be distributed among the neighboring settlers.[1]

The laws promulgated in December, 1512, relating to the system of *encomiendas*, and known as the laws of Burgos, provided that the Indians should be first brought among the Spaniards; that all gentle means should be used towards the *caciques*, to persuade them to come willingly. " Then for every fifty Indians four large huts, fifteen by thirty feet, should be made by their masters." A certain amount of land for growing yuca, yams, and pepper, and a certain number of fowls, should be set aside for the support of each fifty Indians. A chapel

[1] *Documentos inéditos del Archivo de Indias*, i., 239.

should be constructed where prayers might be said both morning and evening. When the holders of *encomiendas* were engaged in mining, the Indians were required to work five months at a time in the mines, with forty days intervening between the two periods, during which they might till the land on their own account. Each year a small amount of money was given to the Indian, with which he might purchase clothes. In each settlement, there were two visitors or inspectors, but inasmuch as they might have *encomiendas,* they could not be expected to judge the system impartially. The *caciques* were permitted to have only six Indians in their service, and the *cacique* and his servants were to be allotted to the Spaniard holding the largest number of Indians of the same tribe.[1]

Whatever may have been the wishes of the crown as to the spread of this system, it became clear very early that the great advantage of it for the conquerors or colonists made inevitable its extension from the islands, where it originated, to the conquered lands of the continent. Nevertheless the crown, by an order dated July 26, 1523, undertook to forbid the granting of *repartimientos* in Mexico, and to revoke those already granted; but the political and economic interests of Cortes and his followers

[1] Watson, i., 73, 74.

constituted an obstruction which could not
readily be removed. In view of the remonstrances, and on the advice of the Council of
the Indies, the order of prohibition was withdrawn. The practice was therefore continued,
and the natives, under the unaccustomed toil
to which they were driven, continued to diminish in numbers. The laws provided by the
crown and the Council of the Indies contained
abundant provisions apparently designed to
promote the material and spiritual well-being
of the Indians, but under the conditions of
communication then existing between Spain
and Mexico, the actual practice in Mexico was
determined rather by the wishes of the local
authorities than by the will of the king of
Spain.

The system of *repartimientos* was also extended to South America. It was carried out
there for the first time by Pizarro in connection
with the founding of the town of San Miguel,
in 1532; but at this time conditionally

" that the new inhabitants might be maintained,
and the Indians instructed in the faith, conforma-
bly to the orders of his majesty, until it should be
decided what was most suitable for the service of
God and of the king, and most advantageous to
the natives."

The next year Charles V. authorized the granting of *encomiendas* in Peru, and by the Law of Succession of 1536, they were granted for two lives. It was provided also that one who lived in another province might hold Indians in this relation, by appointing an agent who should reside in the province with the Indians concerned.

While these measures were being adopted, the Spanish authorities appear not to have been definitely persuaded of the desirability of the system. Under this condition of affairs, Las Casas's power in the advocacy of the liberation of the Indians became especially manifest. Before the council at Valladolid he announced the proposition that the Indians were by nature free; that, under the crown, they were entitled to its protection; and that they " should be immediately declared free, without exception, and forever." The argument that their labor was necessary to the cultivation of the soil and the development of the mines was swept away as of little weight, since it had not been shown that the mines must be developed or the land cultivated, if these things could be done only by the commission of a great wrong.[1]

Las Casas had been a conspicuous figure in Spain during the preceding two reigns, and Charles V. had grown from boyhood with a full appreciation of his strong and disinterested

[1] Herrera, Dec. vii., Lib. vi., Chap. v.

7

character. He had been in the Indies, and
had, probably, a more thorough knowledge of
the public affairs of America than any other
man in Spain. His experience in laboring for
the conversion of the natives, and in peaceably
establishing his dominion over them, enabled
him to speak as one having authority. He
had held an estate with Indian serfs or slaves,
and had liberated them in obedience to his
conviction of the injustice of the relation. His
preaching in favor of liberation was followed
by his celebrated book, *The Destruction of the
Indies*, and by the *Twenty Reasons* why the
Indians should not be given to the Spaniards
in *encomienda*, or vassalage, or made subject to
individuals in any other manner. In 1539, Las
Casas was in Spain, and his great influence was
directed to urging the adoption of a law that
would release the Indians from bondage and
ameliorate their condition. The advocates of
this reform were not stimulated by hopes of
any material advantage for themselves, but
their opponents were moved to resistance by
the prospects of the loss of wealth and power.
Without being able to command the services
of the Indians, they feared the loss of their revenues and a decline in the value of their lands.
Although they might have set up claims for
vested interests destroyed, yet there was no
possibility of recovering an indemnity from

any source. The material interests of Spain herself had already begun to decline, and extensive borrowing to meet emergencies had now become a feature of national policy. The holders of land in America had, therefore, grounds for supposing they would be called to face more or less complete ruin in case the proposed laws were passed and executed. In view of the difficulties of the situation the emperor's advisers were not of one mind. The laws, however, as they were finally issued by the Council of the Indies, were entirely in harmony with the wishes of Las Casas and the other advocates of the liberation of the Indians. They provided, among other things, that after the death of the conquerors, the *repartimientos* of Indians, given to them in *encomienda*, were not to pass to their heirs, but were to be placed under the king; also that all officers of the crown were to renounce their *repartimientos* at once. They provided, moreover, that personal service of the natives was to be entirely abolished, and that the only right to be retained by the *encomenderos* was the right to a moderate tribute.

Don Tello de Sandoval, a member of the Council of the Indies, was appointed to carry the " New Laws " to Mexico. By his instructions he was empowered to take the *residencia* of all the royal officers, including the viceroy

and the members of the audiencia; to exercise
the functions of a judge; to enjoy the rights
and prerogatives of an inquisitor; to extend or
restrict bishoprics; to convene the bishops of
New Spain for the purpose of providing for the
spiritual welfare of the people; to improve the
colleges, hospitals, and churches, and to further
the establishment of new ones; and to have in
hand all matters of importance to either the
crown or the inhabitants.   Knowledge of the
formation and character of the " New Laws "
reached Mexico before the commissioner, and
the Spanish settlers saw themselves threatened
with the immediate loss of the results of all
their toil and adventure.   As feudal lords over
the Indians who had been allotted to them,
and as vassals of the crown, they held positions
which promised not only dignity but wealth;
and these prospects were to be destroyed at a
single blow.   The despair which took possession of the inhabitants was shown by their
resolution to clothe themselves in mourning
robes, as at a funeral, and go out of the city
to meet the messenger of their evil fortunes.
But the viceroy dissuaded them from carrying
out this plan.   On the 8th of March, 1544,
Sandoval arrived at the City of Mexico, and
was almost immediately met with petitions and
remonstrances concerning the publication of
the laws he had come to execute.   But in spite

of the strong and universal opposition of the Spanish settlers, the laws were published in the City of Mexico, March 24, 1544. They were read publicly in the presence of the viceroy, the special commissioner, the judges, and the other royal officials. This action of the authorities, showing a determination on their part to disregard the wishes of the *encomenderos*, raised a storm of indignation, which threatened to break into open revolt. At this point Bishop Zumarraga poured oil on the troubled waters by calling a meeting at the cathedral, and there leading the Spanish settlers to believe that wherever the laws were opposed to the interests of the Spaniards, they would not be enforced. The settlers took hope not only from the address of the bishop, but also from the knowledge that the clergy were holders of important *encomiendas*, and that their interests in them were likely to weaken their natural loyalty to the crown. The ecclesiastics were, with very few exceptions, in favor of continuing the system of *encomiendas*, and opposed to the liberation of the Indians. With the church as an ally, the *encomenderos* had very good grounds for believing their cause was not hopeless.

In view of the great losses that the execution of the " New Laws " would entail on large numbers of the Spanish settlers, and of the resist-

ance to the authorities that might be aroused
by an attempt to enforce them, both Mendoza
and Sandoval saw the necessity of at least de-
laying action. Commissioners representing
the municipality and the religious orders were
sent to Spain to ask the king to revoke at least
those parts of the "New Laws" which threatened the interests of the settlers. By a royal
decree of October 20, 1545, the desired rev-
ocation was granted. This action filled the
Spanish settlers with joy and the enslaved
Indians with despair.

That the attempt to introduce these laws did
not lead to bloodshed or a popular uprising in
Mexico was in large measure due to the wise
discretion of the viceroy, Mendoza. In Peru,
where the first viceroy, Blasco Nuñez de Vela,
undertook to execute them, the outcome was
quite different. The resistance to the proposed
laws assumed the form of a far-reaching rebellion, led by Gonzalo Pizarro, which resulted in
the death of the viceroy and the temporary
suppression of all authority proceeding from
the Spanish crown.

The question concerning the relation of the
Spaniards to the Indians was not easily solved,
and was consequently passed on from decade
to decade. The "New Laws" of 1542 had
proposed a solution, but the end sought had
not been reached. In 1549, Luis de Velasco

was appointed to supersede Mendoza as viceroy
of Mexico. Mendoza proceeded to Cholula
to receive his successor, and there delivered to
the new viceroy information and instructions
concerning the government. During the fifteen
years of Mendoza's rule, order had been established throughout the viceroyalty; revolts and
conspiracies had been suppressed; and even
the agitation caused by the threatened execution
of the " New Laws " had been allayed by their
postponement. The vast regions of the north
had been explored; mines had been discovered and developed; and towns, such as Guadalajara and Zacatecas, had been established.
Mendoza was transferred to Peru, and Velasco
became his successor with the understanding
that he might be recalled at the end of three
years, provided Mendoza wished to return to
Mexico. Mendoza had found it advisable to de-
fer the execution of the "New Laws," but now,
nine years after their formation, Velasco undertook to apply them. In this he was acting
under specific commands from the king. In
July, 1551, the king ordered that all Indian
women made prisoners of war, and all males
under fourteen years of age should be immediately set free, whether they had been brand-
ed as slaves or not. Under this order were
brought also the prisoners taken in the Jalisco
war. If any person held a prisoner of war in

slavery, it devolved upon him to show that he had been taken in a just war, and in accordance with the law, and failing in this the prisoner might go free. This measure encountered vigorous opposition, but it was nevertheless carried, and as a consequence of it a large number of slaves were liberated. By another royal decree, the viceroy and audiencias were forbidden to hold Indians in service, except for wages, and no one might hereafter demand personal service from the Indians in payment of tribute.

Among other measures of reform belonging to this period may be mentioned the effort of the viceroy to prevent the practice of compelling the natives to carry heavy burdens. The clergy as well as the laymen were guilty of this abuse, but it was thought that the clergy could not be accused and corrected without weakening their moral influence with the Indians. While Velasco was viceroy, attempts were made to limit the authority of the *caciques* in their dealings with their followers, preventing them from inflicting capital punishment or corporal mutilations. A little later efforts were made to cause the natives to live in the towns, in order that they might be compelled to adopt habits of industry; and at the same time the succession to *encomiendas* was regulated.

Prior to 1560 the viceroy had been independent of any other constituted authority in
Mexico; his power was limited only by the will
of the king. The audiencia might correspond
directly with the king, but it could not check
or modify the viceroy's decisions. Moved by
jealousy, or by real or fancied wrongs, the
members of the audiencia undertook to under-
mine the king s confidence in Velasco, and thus
curtail his authority. They did not attack him
openly, but led the king to infer that ill-health
had affected the viceroy's mind to such an extent as to impair his discretion and the sound-
ness of his decisions. They demanded that he
should be required to consult some council
before rendering a decision on public affairs;
and they succeeded in persuading the king to
decree that the viceroy should take no action
without the previous advice and consent of the
audiencia. By this means the members of
the audiencia hoped to destroy the viceroy's
power and prestige. But the viceroy was not
without his partisans. The *ayuntamiento* of
Mexico and the majority of the leading Spaniards of the kingdom objected to the project to
pull down and humiliate the head of the government. Yet the party of the audiencia so
far temporarily prevailed that on the death of
Velasco, in 1564, petitions from certain authorities in the City of Mexico were sent to the

king of Spain, asking for the abolition of the
office of viceroy. The petition was naturally
treated as an interference with the king's
prerogatives.

Those who sought the abolition of this office
wished the king to appoint Valderrama governor, and the Marquis del Valle captain-general.
Valderrama, who was then in Mexico as *visitador*, urged that a viceroy should be appointed,
but that he should not be made president of
the audiencia. On the death of the viceroy,
under the law then in force, his power fell into
the hands of the audiencia, but, at the time of
the death of Velasco, the audiencia was subject
to an investigation. This threw the power
practically into the hands of the *visitador ;* but
on the completion of Valderrama's mission and
his return to Spain, all authority was centred
in the audiencia. This body, however, was
not able to command universal respect, as wit-
ness the unrest and conspiracies which disturbed
the interregnum between Velasco and his successor. When, however, the new viceroy,
Don Gaston de Peralta, arrived in 1566, the
audiencia was clearly master of the situation.
The viceroy made light of the conspiracy,
which it was pretended had been put down
with great sacrifice, and by this means aroused
the opposition of the audiencia. In reply to
the viceroy's report to the crown that there

had been no conspiracy, the judges, or members of the audiencia, advanced the charge that the viceroy was indifferent to the welfare of the country and even disloyal. The king determined to make an investigation, and for this purpose sent three commissioners empowered to take possession of the government and return the viceroy to Spain. On the outward voyage, one of the commissioners died, but the other two, Alonso Muñoz and Luis Carrillo, arrived in Mexico and took up the reins of authority. The cruel and arbitrary character of their rule, as directed by Muñoz, roused the subjects in indignation against them, and led the king to depose them. Power then fell once more into the hands of the oidores, and in the brief period of their administration they succeeded in allaying the popular fears that had been excited by the merciless rule of Muñoz and Carrillo. They were relieved, in 1568, by the arrival of the new viceroy, Martin Enriquez de Almansa, who remained in power in Mexico twelve years, or till 1580, when he was transferred to the viceroyalty of Peru.

The efforts to break the power of the viceroy had no important result. The office was firmly established, a kingdom had been set up in America, and after the reign of the viceroy, Almansa, it continued yet two hundred and forty years. The throne of New Spain was

occupied by sixty viceroys, and their average
term of power was four years. At the close of
the period of Spanish rule in America, the
limits of the viceroy's dominion embraced not
only the region to which the name of New
Spain was at first applied, but also the ancient
kingdoms of Michoacan and Galicia, the Cali-
fornias, the peninsula of Yucatan, and various
other provinces which in the course of time
had been drawn together under the viceregal
government.

CHAPTER V

THE ESTABLISHMENT OF SPANISH POWER
IN PERU

IN the growth of civilization in South America, certain districts which had an individual colonial existence have become the seats of independent states. The most conspicuous of these regions are Peru, the valley of La Plata, the territory of Chile, Venezuela, and those portions of the continent now occupied by the republics of Colombia and Ecuador. For many decades Lima, in Peru, was the social and political capital of South America.

The first important step towards carrying Spanish institutions to Peru was the formation of the famous contract between Pizarro and his associates. Before this contract was formed, Pizarro and Almagro had made separate voyages southward from Panama. On these voyages, however, no great discoveries were made, nor the expected riches acquired. Yet

during these voyages the rumors which the
leaders had heard previously became more
definite, and confirmed their belief in the existence of a kingdom of abundant wealth farther
towards the south.

The parties involved in this contract were
the two captains, Pizarro and Almagro, and
the ecclesiastic, Fernando de Luque. Luque
agreed to advance the funds for the undertaking, while Almagro and Pizarro pledged themselves to carry out the plan of conquest. The
conquered territory, the *repartimientos*, the
treasures of gold, silver, and precious stones,
and the spoils of every kind, were to be divided
equally among the three partners. Even one
third of all revenues derived from grants which
the crown might make to either Pizarro or Almagro should be enjoyed by Luque, and might
be transmitted by him to his heirs or legal
representatives. The risk in the enterprise was
borne by the two military leaders, who agreed,
in case of failure, to reimburse Luque for his
advances, and for this purpose pledged whatever property they might possess. They
agreed, moreover, to allow the contract to
have the force of a judgment issued against
them by a court of justice. The contract was
subscribed by Luque on the 10th of March,
1526. It was duly attested by witnesses, one
of whom signed for Pizarro, and another for

Almagro, it being affirmed that neither of the captains was able to write his name. A marked religious tone pervades this document, which constitutes the basis of a gigantic scheme of spoliation, and it was solemnly sworn to and acknowledged in the name of God and the Holy Evangelists.[1] In this transaction Luque was only the agent of Gaspar de Espinosa, who had had an important part in the conquest and settlement of Tierra Firme, and had held the office of alcalde in Darien. To him, therefore, and not to Luque, was due the stipulated one third part of the proceeds of the projected conquest. The first expedition made under this contract verified the rumors concerning the abundance of gold that might be found in Peru; but the leaders thought themselves too weak to undertake the conquest, and returned to Panama without the expected profits for Luque's investment. The difficulty encountered in getting funds for a subsequent expedition might be regarded as evidence that the captains did not make good to Luque the loss by the first voyage under the contract. Fifteen hundred ducats were, however, raised to enable Pizarro to go to Spain, and appeal directly to the king for aid.

Pizarro left Panama for Spain in the spring

[1] The text of this contract is given as Appendix No. vi. in Prescott, *Conquest of Peru*, ii., 486–490.

of 1528.   Neither his history nor his character
was such as to suggest the typical Spanish
courtier, yet his appearance before the king,
the story of his undertakings and privations,
and the zeal which he had displayed in the
cause of the crown made a deep impression.
On the 26th of July, 1529, was issued the
Capitulation which granted to Pizarro the powers and privileges he enjoyed in carrying on
the conquest of Peru.   In accordance with this
decree, Pizarro and his associates were permitted to continue their conquests at their own
expense; and they were, moreover, granted the
territory of Peru, extending on the sea from
Santiago two hundred leagues southward.   Of
this region, Pizarro was made governor and
captain-general for life, with an annual salary
of 1820 dollars, which was to be paid from the
king's revenues derived from the lands in
question.   Out of this salary he was required
to pay every year an alcalde, ten squires, thirty
peons, a physician, and an apothecary.   He
was given also the title of *adelantado* and
alguacil mayor of the province of Peru.   In
agreement with the royal officers of the province, he was permitted to construct and maintain four fortresses in such places as he might
find convenient.   He was permitted also to
distribute the Indians among his followers
under the law of *encomiendas*, and control the

affairs of his province with that practically
absolute authority implied in his title of captain-general. Diego de Almagro was made
commandant of the fortress at Tumbez, with
an annual salary of two hundred and fifty dollars and five hundred dollars towards expenses.
He was at the same time raised to the rank of
a nobleman, and given all the honors and privileges which that title conveyed.

Father Luque was made bishop of Tumbez
and protector of the Indians of Peru, and was
provided with an annual salary of one thousand
ducats. Bartolomé Ruiz was granted the position of grand pilot of the South Sea, with a
salary of about one hundred and ninety dollars
a year, to be paid, like all the salaries granted
through this instrument, from the proceeds of
the lands conquered. Other companions of
Pizarro were given either minor offices or titles
of distinction. In order to increase the population of the province, certain restrictions on
emigration were removed, and the ordinary
laws of taxation were relaxed in favor of the
settlers. The tax on the precious metals was
reduced to one tenth for a term of six years.
It was provided that at the expiration of this
period the tax of one tenth should be changed
to one ninth, and thus increased year by year
by one point till it should again reach one
fifth.

8

" It was expressly enjoined on Pizarro to observe the existing regulations for the good government and protection of the natives ; and he was required to carry out with him a specified number of ecclesiastics, with whom he was to take counsel in the conquest of the country, and whose efforts were to be dedicated to the service and conversion of the Indians ; while lawyers and attorneys, on the other hand, whose presence was considered as boding ill to the harmony of the new settlements, were strictly prohibited from setting foot in them.

" Pizarro, on his part, was bound, in six months from the date of the instrument, to raise a force, well equipped for the service, of two hundred and fifty men, of whom one hundred might be drawn from the colonies ; and the government engaged to furnish some trifling assistance in the purchase of artillery and military stores. Finally, he was to be prepared, in six months after his return to Panama, to leave that port and embark on his expedition." [1]

The events of Pizarro's march into the interior of Peru from the region of Tumbez are already familiar. It is necessary here simply to emphasize the efforts made to establish the forms and institutions of civilized society. The first step in this direction was the foundation of the municipality of San Miguel in the valley of Tangarala, about one hundred miles south of Tumbez. The men left at Tumbez

[1] Prescott, *Conquest of Peru*, i., 305–307 ; also ii., 490–497.

were ordered to take up their residence there; buildings were constructed from the timber of the forests and stone from the neighboring quarries; and a municipal government was organized in a form prescribed by law, consisting of regidores, alcaldes, and such other civil officers as were found necessary. To each settler was allotted a portion of the surrounding territory, and a certain number of Indians who might be required to cultivate it; for as, according to Pizarro's secretary, it was

" evident that the colonists could not support themselves without the services of the Indians, the ecclesiastics and the leaders of the expedition all agreed that a *repartimiento* of the natives would serve the cause of religion, and tend greatly to their spiritual welfare, since they would thus have the opportunity of being initiated in the true faith." [1]

The original site having been found to be unhealthy, the town was moved to the bank of the Piura, where it stands to-day, the oldest town in Peru founded by Europeans.

After the death of Atahualpa and the surrender of Cuzco, Pizarro organized a municipal government in the ancient capital. It was composed of two alcaldes and eight regidores. Among the latter were Gonzalo and Juan Pizarro, brothers of the captain-general. The

[1] Quoted by Prescott, i., 358.

oath of office was administered to the members of the new government on the 24th of March, 1534. Spaniards were invited to become residents of Cuzco, and Pizarro, as governor of Peru, offered them certain houses and lands which had come into his possession as a result of the conquest. Pizarro also laid the foundation of an ecclesiatical organization, and Father Valverde was made bishop of Cuzco. One side of the plaza was selected as a site for the cathedral, and monasteries rose in the place of edifices formerly devoted to the Indian worship, and the ecclesiastics who came with Pizarro and those who came as later reinforcements carried on with zeal the work of converting the Indians, and, on the part of some of the missionaries, with a disinterested devotion to their spiritual welfare.

The claims of Pizarro to northern Peru were disputed by Alvarado, who landed in March, 1534, in the bay of Caraques, and with great suffering and loss crossed the Andes to Quito. A conflict between Alvarado and Pizarro appeared to be imminent, but was avoided by an agreement in which the governor promised to pay Alvarado one hundred thousand *pesos de oro*, and received from him his ships, his troops, and all his stores.[1]

The foundation of Lima in January, 1535, to

[1] It was " arranged that Alvarado should cede his army to

be the capital of Peru, prepared the way for a
struggle between the old and the new centres
of power. As a consequence of the visit of
Hernando Pizarro to the court of Spain in 1534,
the boundary of Francisco Pizarro's jurisdiction
was removed seventy leagues towards the south,
and Almagro was empowered to occupy and
hold the region extending from the southern
line of Pizarro's dominion southward two hundred leagues. There was no lack of defi-
niteness in the terms of the grants to the two
commanders, but for want of accurate measure-
ments it was still doubtful to whom belonged
the ancient capital, Cuzco. The conflict which
threatened to grow out of this controversy was
temporarily set aside by a compact between
Pizarro and Almagro, in which they agreed to
observe towards one another such conduct as
civilized men have supposed was demanded by
common decency. Neither should malign the
other, nor injure him with respect to his repu-
tation, his person, or his property. They
swore to carry out strictly the terms of the
present agreement; that neither should report
or write to the king without the knowledge of

Pizarro and Almagro, and that they should give him a hundred
thousand golden ducats, on condition that he should go away
and never more return to that kingdom. In this manner
Alvarado departed from Peru with four servants, and returned
to Guatamala in good spirits and contented."—Benzoni, *History of the New World*, 154.

the other; and that all the profits and interests
which should be acquired by future conquests
and discoveries should be shared equally by
both. Upon either of the parties who should
act contrary to this compact, they invoked the
Divine wrath, and prayed that Heaven might
visit him with the loss of honor, family, and
property in this life, and with eternal perdition
in the life to come. The agreement was confirmed by a solemn oath taken on the sacrament, recorded by a notary, and attested by a
large number of witnesses.[1]

Shortly after the formation of this contract
Almagro entered upon the conquest of Chile,
and Pizarro returned to the administration of
his province and the building of his capital.
On the return of Hernando Pizarro from Spain,
he brought to the governor a royal patent conferring upon him the title of *Marques de los
Atavillos*, and the grant permitting him to extend his territory seventy leagues towards the
south. By the commissioners Francisco Pizarro
was now assured that Cuzco undoubtedly fell
within his jurisdiction. When, therefore, Almagro returned from Chile and seized this city,
the conditions of hostility were clearly established, in spite of the solemn stipulations of
the recently formed contract.

[1] Prescott, ii., 35 ; also ii., 509, 511 for the text of the contract, which was dated June 12, 1535.

In this manner was introduced the first civil war, which resulted in Almagro's defeat at the battle of Las Salinas, his subsequent execution, and the spread of disorder and confusion over the whole country. The ancient government had been overthrown, and in view of the conflicts between the Spaniards and the Indians and the civil wars arising from the jealousy of the Spanish leaders, the province appeared to be on the verge of hopeless anarchy. As a means of averting the impending danger, Pizarro established settlements in the disaffected districts. These were called cities, and had, in fact, the form of a municipal corporation, but they were in reality military colonies for the maintenance of order and the Spanish authority. Settlers were attracted to them by the protection which they afforded, and by the grants of land offered, and they grew rapidly to be not merely military outposts, but also centres of local commerce. Among the settlements of this time, which later became conspicuous cities, were La Plata, in the district of Charcas, and Arequipa, near the coast.

The execution of Almagro did not put an end to civil conflict. The Almagro faction survived, and found a leader in the son of the executed commander. Goaded to action by their poverty and their desire for revenge, the members of this faction formed a conspiracy, assassinated Pizarro, took possession of Cuzco, and demanded that the young Almagro should be recognized as governor of Peru. That phase of the early civil wars of Peru, which followed these events, under the leadership of Vaca de Castro, on the one side, and the young Almagro on the other, culminated in the battle of Chupas. Almagro was overthrown and imprisoned, and a little later was executed in Cuzco. The threatened uprising under Gonzalo Pizarro, who had returned from his expedition into the region of the upper Amazon, was averted, and Vaca de Castro set himself to order and reform the administration of the country. He encouraged the restless cavaliers to undertake exploring expeditions into the distant country of the Rio de la Plata; he sought to establish better laws for the province; he endeavored to ameliorate the condition of the Indians; and he founded schools in which they might be taught the doctrines of Christianity. He facilitated communication between the different parts of the province by requiring the *caciques* to provide supplies for the *tambos* in their neighborhood, which would take away from the Spaniards their excuse for plundering the natives. He attempted to bring about a better relation between the Indians and the Spaniards, and to this end sought to readjust the affairs of the *repartimientos,*

but in this undertaking he touched the most
deep-seated abuse of Peru or of Spanish
America. The Spaniards held to the privilege
of keeping the Indians in service with great
tenacity. They regarded it as their most valu-
able reward for their labors and dangers of discovery and explorations, and at the same time
as the necessary foundation of their prosperity.
The thought that the abolition of this privilege
would entail their material ruin led them to
oppose vigorously any project to overthrow
the system of *repartimientos*. It was this spirit
that resisted the proposed introduction of the
" New Laws," which had been formed under
the influence of Las Casas.

These laws were intended to apply to all of
the Spanish possessions in America, and had
their basis in the asserted right of the Indians
to liberty. It was not proposed that these
laws should annul any contract which the government of the Indies had made with the conquerors, or set aside any privilege which had
been previously granted. All persons who
lawfully held Indian slaves might continue to
hold them for the period of their lives; but it
was required that at the death of the existing
proprietors the slaves should revert to the
crown. They should, moreover, be forfeited
by holders under whom they had suffered
neglect or ill-usage; and, according to a still

more sweeping clause, they should be forfeited
" by all public functionaries, or such as had
held offices under the government; by ecclesiastics and religious corporations; and, lastly,
by all who had taken a criminal part in the
feuds of Almagro and Pizarro." [1]

In order to put an end to confusion and provide a strong government in Peru, it was determined to establish at Lima a viceroy and royal
audiencia, through whom the " New Laws "
might be carried into effect.   At the same time
the audiencia of Panama was abolished and its
functions transferred to the government of
Peru.

The Spanish settlers of Peru, with remarkable
unanimity, felt that the enforcement of these
laws would deprive them of whatever material
advantages and prospects they possessed.
They appealed to the government of Peru to
protect them against the destructive measures
of the Spanish court; but when they discovered
that a new government was to be established,
and that it was to be especially commissioned
to enforce these laws, the way of self-preserva-
tion and defence appeared to lead to rebellion.
They turned to Gonzalo Pizarro with the demand that he should become their leader.   As
the last of the brothers of that family remaining
in the province, he was regarded as the bearer

[1] Prescott, ii., 254.

of the heroism that had been displayed in the conquest, and the natural defender of the interests of the conquerors. The task of allaying the incipient rebellion and of introducing the " New Laws " was confided by Charles V to Blasco Nuñez de Vela,[1] who left Spain November 3, 1543, and landed at Nombre de Dios about the middle of the following January. He was attended by the four judges of the new audiencia, and by a numerous retinue befitting his exalted position and viceregal power. The contrasted positions of the two opposing leaders appear when we reflect on their respective attitudes towards the people of the province. Pizarro left his mining operations at Potosi to lead the rebellion, on the demand of the settlers; Blasco Nuñez, in his arbitrary exercise of power, not only ran counter to the wishes of his subjects, even before he arrived in his kingdom, but overrode the decisions of the audiencia and disregarded the will of every

---

[1] The new viceroy had been Inspector-General of the Guards of Castile. " In character he was an upright, narrow-minded, sincere, intemperate, loyal man. He was a favorite courtier of Charles the Fifth's, having hitherto executed his majesty's commands with a loving obedience and great exactitude. He was handsome, of noble presence, skilled in knightly arts, very pious and very harsh." He left Spain in November, 1543, and on the 18th of June, 1546, he was killed in the battle of Añaquito, in which the rebellion against the " New Laws " and his administration was triumphant.

constituted authority. His lack of tact was revealed in his complete repudiation of the policy of conciliation. " He had come," he said, " not to tamper with the laws, nor to discuss their merits, but to execute them,—and execute them he would, to the letter, whatever might be the consequence." [1] From this utterance the members of the audiencia clearly discerned that their will was not to be made effective when it traversed the will of the viceroy. Owing to the illness of one of the judges, the viceroy entered Peru without the audiencia. Reports of his opinions and arbitrary acts had preceded him, and the magnificent display which attended his progress to the capital, while it may have overawed a few, did little to set aside the evil forebodings of the many, or to check the growing spirit of rebellion.

The most important events in the viceroy's brief career in America were his arrival in Lima, his installation as viceroy of Peru, the announcement of his determination to maintain the ordinances, the murder of Carbajal, the increased indignation of the people, the campaign of Pizarro, the banishment of the viceroy, Gonzalo Pizarro's gorgeous triumphal entry into Lima, and the proclamation of the victor as governor and captain-general of Peru. The

[1] See Prescott, ii., 261.

second part of this brief period was marked by
the establishment of Pizarro's administration,
the reappearance of Blasco Nuñez, the raising
of his standard at San Miguel, the advance of
Pizarro towards this town, the disastrous flight
of Blasco Nuñez towards the north, and his
defeat and death on the plains of Añaquito.
After this last event, Gonzalo Pizarro's authority extended over the whole of Peru; his power
was everywhere acknowledged, from Quito on
the north to the border of Chile on the south,
and even the towns on the Isthmus, which
constituted the key to the Pacific, had fallen
into his hands. He was apparently in a favorable position to assume sovereign power, and
to erect in Peru an independent monarchy.
And among the followers of Pizarro there were
some who urged him to pursue this course; but
he appears to have hesitated to strike directly
at the authority of the crown. The practical
problem which Peruvian affairs at this time
presented to the Spanish court, required for its
proper solution the most careful treatment.
The difficulties were very great. Soldiers had
to be transported across the Atlantic. The
Isthmus was held by Pizarro, and enormous
obstacles stood in the way of reaching Peru by
any other route. Pizarro's vessels commanded
the Pacific, and even if the royalist forces succeeded in landing they would be greatly hand-

icapped, as compared with the veterans of
Pizarro, by an unknown country and an un-
tried climate. There was also danger that the
new troops would be allured by the expectation
of rich booty or the spoils of the mines, and,
disregarding their allegiance to the king, ally
themselves with the forces in insurrection.
The crown had, therefore, to adopt some other
policy than uncompromising coercion, or run
the risk of losing Peru completely.

In this critical state of affairs, a plan of conciliation was adopted, and Pedro de la Gasca
was commissioned to undertake the difficult
task of bringing Peru to acknowledge and maintain allegiance to the crown.   Gasca left Spain
for Peru in May, 1546. As a youth he had
been a student in the seminary of Alcalá de
Henares, and later at Salamanca. He had
been a member of the Council of the Inquisition, and had held the responsible post of
visitador of the kingdom of Valencia. When,
therefore, he was appointed to the important
undertaking in Peru, he was known to have
already managed difficult cases with great skill
and discretion.   He accepted the appointment,
and seeing the necessity of independent action
in possible emergencies, without being compelled to wait for instructions from the court,
he demanded that he should be clothed with
all of the authority of the sovereign within the

field of his activity. This apparently extravagant demand was willingly granted by the emperor; and, under the simple title of President of the Audiencia, he was empowered to do whatever the king might do under the given conditions. He was at the head of every department of the administration; he might raise troops, appoint and remove officers, and declare war; he might exercise the royal prerogative of pardoning offences; and was especially commissioned to grant an amnesty to all who had been engaged in the rebellion. He was authorized to revoke the ordinances which had caused the popular uprising and overthrow of Blasco Nuñez; and, returning to the earlier practice, might make *repartimientos*, or confirm those which had been previously made. In accordance with his expressed wish, he was granted no specific salary, but might make any demands on the treasuries of Peru and Panama.

When Gasca landed at Nombre de Dios, in the plain garb of a simple ecclesiastic, those who received him were not then aware that he was the bearer of the essential powers of an absolute prince. Yet the policy which he proposed to carry out was a policy of pardon and conciliation. He wrote to Pizarro from Panama, forwarding to him at the same time the conciliatory letter of the emperor. He indicated his determination to concede all that Pizarro had contended for. When the reply to these letters was received, it was in the form of a letter from the inhabitants of Lima, dated October 14, 1546, congratulating the president on his arrival, but expressing regret that he had come so late, after all the troubles of the country had been settled, and peace had been established under the rule of Pizarro. At the same time Gasca was informed that an embassy was on its way to the Spanish court to ask that Pizarro might be confirmed as governor of Peru. It was, moreover, intimated that the presence of the president would be likely to renew the social disturbance, and might cost him his life. The interview between Aldana, of the embassy, and the president, in which the former learned the extent of Gasca's powers and the nature of the concessions to Pizarro and his followers, changed materially the prospects of both parties. Aldana abandoned his mission to Spain, accepted the offered pardon, agreed to support the president, and recommended to Pizarro to pursue the same course. The next important step in the progress of Gasca's cause was the surrender of the fleet. Hinojosa and his officers gave up their commissions into the hands of the president as the representative of the Spanish crown. In return, the president, in the name of the crown,

pardoned all past offences, restored to the officers their commissions, and greeted them as the
loyal subjects of the emperor. By this politic
act, Pizarro's power on the ocean was transferred to the president undiminished.

With the fleet in Gasca's possession, the
way to Peru was open to him, and the later
events of his contest with the insurgents followed one another in rapid succession. After
Pizarro had rejected the peaceful overtures of
the president and determined to appeal to the
decision of force, there was no alternative for
Gasca but to accept the challenge. In the
campaign which followed, the advantage at
first appeared to be on the side of the insurgents. At the battle of Huarina, the royalist
forces, under Centeno, were defeated and scattered in hopeless confusion, while in the final
contest near Cuzco, at the battle of Xaquixa-
guana, the followers of Pizarro were routed
and his cause was lost. Pizarro and Carbajal
were executed. Confiscated property was distributed among the victors, and the president
undertook to reform the administration. He
limited the amount of service that might be
demanded of the natives. He provided that
they should not be compelled to change their
residence from one climate to another, thus
avoiding the great suffering that had been imposed upon them by carrying them from the
9

hot regions of the coast to work in the mines
in the cold regions of the mountains.

About three years after his first landing in
Peru, Gasca prepared to return to Spain. He
entrusted the government to the royal audiencia, and embarked for Spain, by way of
Panama, in January, 1550. Concerning the
character of Gasca and his career in Peru, the
most varied opinions have been expressed by
different writers. Prescott sums up his achievements quite in the tone of eulogy. According
to this writer, when Gasca landed,

" he found the colony in a state of anarchy, or
rather organized rebellion under a powerful and
popular chief. He came without funds or forces
to support him. The former he procured through
the credit which he established in his good faith ;
the latter he won over by argument and persuasion
from the very persons to whom they had been confided by his rival. Thus he turned the arms of
that rival against himself. By a calm appeal to
reason he wrought a change in the hearts of the
people ; and, without costing a drop of blood to a
single loyal subject, he suppressed a rebellion which
had menaced Spain with the loss of the wealthiest
of her provinces. He had punished the guilty,
and in their spoils found the means to recompense
the faithful. He had, moreover, so well husbanded
the resources of the country, that he was enabled
to pay off the large loan he had negotiated with
the merchants of the colony, for the expenses of

the war, exceeding nine hundred thousand *pesos de
oro*. Nay, more, by his economy he had saved a
million and a half of ducats for the government,
which for some years had received nothing from
Peru ; and he now proposed to carry back this
acceptable treasure to swell the royal coffers. All
this had been accomplished without the cost of
outfit or salary, or any charge to the crown except
that of his own frugal expenditure. The country
was now in a state of tranquillity. Gasca felt that
his work was done ; and that he was free to gratify
his natural longing to return to his native land."[1]

Markham, on the other hand, in his *History
of Peru*, calls President Gasca " the ignoble
conqueror " and " the cowardly priest," and
suggests that after the death of Gonzalo Pizarro, " the colonists had little cause to rejoice
at the change of masters." Referring to the
president's conduct after victory, he says that

" at length, sated with blood, Gasca left Cuzco and
went to a small village in the neighborhood, with
Archbishop Loaysa of Lima, to arrange the distribution of grants of land and Indians among his followers. He retired into this seclusion to avoid the
importunities of friends. Having completed his
work, he sent to announce his awards at Cuzco,
and they caused a howl of rage and disappointed
greed. He himself went down to Lima by the least
frequented route, and when a positive order from

[1] Prescott, ii., 457.

the emperor arrived that all personal service from the Indians should be prohibited, he suspended its publication until he was safe out of Peru."

Markham does not find the tranquillity of which Prescott writes, nor does the president's task appear to him to have been completed. The country was left, he says, " in the greatest confusion, and all the most difficult administrative points to be settled by others."

The government of Peru remained in the hands of the audiencia somewhat more than a year and a half, from January, 1550, to September, 1551, or till the arrival of the second viceroy, Don Antonio de Mendoza. For fifteen years Mendoza had been viceroy of Mexico, and it was owing to his great prudence that Mexico had been able to avoid a civil war at the time of the proposed introduction of the " New Laws "; for, standing between the specific command of the king and the unyielding holders of Indian slaves, he assumed the responsibility of so mitigating the law " that every man possessing slaves should each year, according to a certain rate, liberate twenty." Considering this conduct, Benzoni remarks that " if Blasco Nuñez Vela, on going as viceroy to Peru with similar orders, had acted in this manner, he would not have come to the end he did." [1]

[1] *History of the New World*, 58.

The death of Mendoza, in July, 1552, threw the government of Peru once more into the hands of the audiencia. In addition to the dissatisfaction caused by Gasca's awards of confiscated property, the audiencia had to seek to allay another discontent caused by the ordinance which deprived the conquerors of the personal services of the natives. The incipient rebellion which sprung from these grievances was suppressed in Charcas by Alvarado, but under the leadership of Francisco Hernandez Giron, the uprising assumed a more threatening form. Through a conspiracy Giron got possession of the city of Cuzco, and set up there his authority. His followers increased in numbers rapidly. The soldiers who had been scattered by Gasca's victory, and the discontented of every sort gathered about his standard. He professed not to be in rebellion against the crown, but appeared only to redress wrongs and bring the country back to tranquillity. He addressed the principal cities, the leading captains, and the audiencia of Lima, attempting to persuade them not to be disturbed by his activity, as he was aiming at the public good, and to induce the king, in ordering the government of Peru, to consult the welfare of the people. At the same time he sent troops to Guamanga and to take possession of Arequipa. In the conflict which en-

sued, the legitimate forces were in one respect
at a disadvantage as compared with the insurgents.   They had no single leader whom they
were willing to entrust with the conduct of the
campaign, and the members of the audiencia
were so suspicious of one another that they
determined to take the field together.   If a
collegiate executive in civil affairs may be
found advisable sometimes, a committee has
never shown itself especially well adapted to
military leadership.   But in spite of Giron's
brilliant prospects after the victory of Chu-
quinga, his cause suffered the disadvantage of
not being the cause of the legitimate government.   Blockaded in his stronghold at Pucara,
and not being able to induce his opponents to
fight, Giron saw no hope but in flight.   He
was, however, captured and brought to Lima,
and executed, and with his death, in the beginning of 1555, the early civil wars of Peru
were ended.

At the close of the civil wars there were
about eight thousand Spaniards in Peru.   Of
these, four hundred and eighty-nine held grants
of land and Indians, and about one thousand
others occupied official positions or lived on
their estates; but a large part of the whole
number may be described as adventurers; they
desired to live without labor, and the peace
and order of a settled society were scarcely

compatible with their purposes. With this
population, Peru did not offer an attractive
field for the work of administration. The
Spaniards appear to have taken this view of
it ; for two noblemen to whom the king, in
1555, offered the position of viceroy in succession refused it; but it was finally accepted,
with reluctance, however, by Don Andres Hurtado de Mendoza, Marquis of Cañete. He was
appointed for six years with an annual salary of
forty thousand ducats. Among the first measures proposed by Mendoza were those to expel
from the country some of the more dangerous
characters, to engage others in exploring unknown regions, and to prohibit persons from
going to Peru, except under certain specified
conditions. Mendoza assumed the duties of
office in Lima, in June, 1556. His orders
issued after his arrival in Peru, as well as his
policy outlined in Seville, indicate that he
proposed to rule with a firm hand. He decreed that the Spaniards should be confined to
the districts in which they lived, except as
permitted by the authorities to remove to
other places. He organized a special guard of
four hundred, and brought the artillery from
all parts of the province, and ordered it kept
under his immediate control, at the same time
putting an end to the practice, in accordance
with which corregidors in their several districts

had been in the habit of keeping soldiers under their commands. He then called the members of the audiencia to account for their conduct of affairs before his appointment. They had been in contention among themselves, and had led the forces in the field instead of performing their proper duties at the capital. He called to Lima the unruly spirits who were likely to cause disturbance, and banished them to Spain or Chile. Tomas Vasquez and Martin de Robles, who had been convicted of previous offences and pardoned, the former by the audiencia and the latter by Gasca, were both beheaded by the order of Mendoza. His rule was unquestionably severe, but it was effective. It put an end to the lawlessness with which the country had been afflicted for a decade.

During the administration of Hurtado de Mendoza, who was accompanied by his family, the viceregal court was set up, and Lima assumed the forms and ceremonies of civilized society, and became the social centre of South America. The pretentious display of the viceroy's court was not without influence in maintaining order among colonists who had been accustomed to look to the ceremonious court of Madrid as the source of authority that could not be disregarded.

The viceroy had undertaken the government of Peru with the assurance that he would be

supported by the court of Madrid in all measures that were found to be necessary to establish public order. But his expectations in this
regard were not realized. Spaniards whom he
had banished found their way to Spain and
persuaded the new king, Philip II., that the
severe measures of Mendoza were unnecessary
and constituted a hindrance to the progress of
Peru and to the development of Spanish interests in the colony; and the infrequency and
difficulty of communication between Spain and
America made it impossible for the king to be
kept fully informed on Peruvian affairs, or for
charges made in Spain against royal officers in
Peru to be readily refuted. In this case Philip
appears to have taken action on one-sided information, and superseded the viceroy by the
appointment of Don Diego de Acevedo y Zuñiga, Count of Nieva, as his successor. But
Mendoza died before the arrival of the new
viceroy. His government had lasted nearly
five years, and during this period he had succeeded in establishing peace among the inhabitants of Peru, and had laid the foundations
of an orderly administration.

The demand that Peru should return a large
revenue to Spain stood constantly in the way
of establishing a good government for Peru.
From the Spanish point of view, that was
likely to be pronounced a good government

which gave Spain the largest revenue, while from the Peruvian point of view it might possibly appear to have few points of advantage. Mendoza sent to Spain 684,287 ducats, but there was always a demand for more; for Spain in her decline towards bankruptcy was practically insatiable, and the management of Spanish-American affairs from the side of Spain was largely determined by the hope of increasing the revenues of the home government.

At the close of the brief rule of the Count of Nieva, the title of viceroy of Peru was temporarily suspended. His successor, Lope Garcia de Castro, who entered Lima in September, 1564, was known as governor and captain-general. He was president of the audiencia, and remained at the head of the government for five years. During this time peace was maintained among the inhabitants, and steps were taken towards perfecting the administrative organization by dividing the territory into districts, in each of which power should be exercised by a corregidor. In this period, moreover, certain customs duties were established, and the quicksilver mines of Huancavelica were opened. In spite of the prohibition of trade between Spanish-American colonies, or states, a part of the product of these mines was later transported to Mexico to be used in reducing the silver ores of that country.

On the retirement of Garcia de Castro, in
November, 1569, the title of viceroy was revived, and Don Francisco de Toledo became
the fifth viceroy of Peru.　He came apparently
resolved on the plan of his work as viceroy.
This plan involved, among other things, the
making of a new code of ordinances for the
government of the viceroyalty, the extermination of the Inca dynasty, and the regulation of
the ecclesiastical affairs in such a manner that
the power of the priest would supplement that
of the viceroy.　An important part of Toledo's code, which was known as the *Libro de
Tasas*, consisted of provisions relating to local
government.　The division of the territory and
the organization of local authorities, which had
been made under previous rulers, were in this
code described and confirmed.　The corregidor
was recognized as the governor of a district
called a *corregimiento*.　Municipal governments
were established consisting of one or more
alcaldes and a number of regidores, varying
according to the size or importance of the city.
By the rules of the code, an attempt was made
not only to fix the duties of the several officers,
but also to regulate the affairs of trade.　The
viceroy desired also to revive or maintain certain institutions that belonged to the governmental system of the Incas, particularly that
part of the Inca organization which was estab-

lished for maintaining the roads and stations, and the organization of the Indians under *caciques*. One practical advantage of recognizing the superiority of the *cacique* was that he might use his authority in collecting tribute from the Indians on behalf of the viceroy's government. The Indians were not only obliged to pay tribute, but also to render personal service in the manufactories and on farms. This service, called the *mita*, was demanded of one seventh part of the adult Indian male population, exclusive of those employed in the mines. In spite of all laws intended to regulate the payment of wages and the distance the Indians might be taken from their homes, the *mita* remained an instrument of extreme oppression. Another form of slavery was that in which the so-called *yanaconas* were involved. These rendered for the most part household service, and for this they were given food, clothing, and a payment of their tribute by the master.

The second point of the viceroy's policy, the extermination of the Inca dynasty, was carried out by the unprovoked murder of Tupac Amaru and a number of his devoted followers.

In ordering the affairs of the church, a priest was established in each village, and charged to teach the Indians the doctrines of Christianity and to destroy all evidence of their ancient worship. But the great blessing of the new religion brought with it pecuniary burdens in the form of fees for christenings, masses, and burials.

The thirteen years of Toledo's administration in Peru ended in 1581. On the 28th of September he surrendered the government to Don Martin Enriquez, who had been viceroy in Mexico, and who carried to his new position somewhat of experience in American affairs. In the brief period before his death, on the 15th of March, 1583, he had only opportunity to show that in the conduct of the administration he was disposed to proceed along lines indicated by his predecessor.

After the death of Enriquez, Peru remained without a viceroy till the arrival of the Count of Villar, in November, 1586, a period of a little more than three years, and during this time the governmental power rested in the hands of the audiencia. When the Count of Villar took up the reins of government in Peru, he was old and inefficient, and, in 1590, gave way to Don Garcia Hurtado de Mendoza, the son of an earlier viceroy. Mendoza had been at the head of the government of Chile, and thus entered upon his undertaking in Peru with the prestige of a successful ruler. He landed at Callao, on the 6th of January, 1590, and made his solemn entry into the capital.[1]

[1] The ceremony attending the reception of the viceroy at

Conspicuous among the hindrances to good government which the viceroy encountered, was Spain's demand for gold and silver. The Spaniards in Spain who were interested in Peru wished undoubtedly the establishment of a beneficent political order and the conversion of the natives, provided the attainment of these ends was found to be consistent with drawing from the colony the greatest possible revenue. In obtaining this revenue, the Indians were sent to labor and perish by the hundred in the mines, and they were everywhere subjected to a burdensome tribute. The second Marquis of Cañete sent to Spain 1,500,000 ducats, besides plate and jewels; and in 1591, 311,257 Indians paid tribute to their feudal superiors, or the *encomenderos*, amounting to 1,434,420 ducats. In the import and export duties, and in the *alcabala*, the viceregal government found its main sources of income. The latter, consisting of a tax of two per cent. on all provisions sold in the market, and a tax of five per cent. on cocoa, was an almost intolerable burden, and in some cases drove the people to insurrection, as in the revolt of Quito.

After holding the position of viceroy for somewhat more than six years, Mendoza re-

the capital has been described, as it appeared later, by George Juan and Antonio de Ulloa in *A Voyage to South America,* ii., 46.

turned to Spain, and was succeeded, in 1596, by Don Luis de Velasco, Marquis of Salinas, who was viceroy of Peru till his removal to Mexico, in 1604.

By the beginning of the seventeenth century, the political affairs of Peru had fallen into a settled order. The viceroys followed one another without greatly disturbing the monotonous routine. If there were sometimes brief periods between the going of one viceroy and the coming of his successor, the governmental power of the kingdom fell, in the meantime, into the hands of the audiencia. The following is a list of the viceroys who ruled in Peru in the seventeenth century, between 1604 and 1705:

Count of Monterey	1604–1605
Juan de Mendoza,	
Marquis of Montes Claros . .	1607–1615
Francisco de Borja Aragon,	
Prince of Esquilache . . .	1615–1621
Diego Fernandez de Cordova,	
Marquis of Guadalcazar . .	1622–1629
Luis Geronimo de Cabrera,	
Count of Chinchon . . .	1629–1639
Pedro de Toledo y Leyva,	
Marquis of Mancera . . .	1639–
Count of Salvatierra	–1655
Luis Henriquez de Guzman,	
Count of Alba de Liste . .	1655–1661

Diego Benavides y de la Cueva,	
Count of Santistevan . . .	1661–1666
Pedro Fernandez de Castro Andrade y	
Portugal, Count of Lemos .	1667–1672
Balthasar de la Cueva,	
Count of Castellar . . .	1672–1678
Melchor de Liñan y Cisneros . .	1678–1681
Melchor de Navarra y Ròcaful,	
Duke of La Palata . . .	1681–1689
Melchor Portocarrero Laso de la Vega,	
Count of Monclova . . .	1689–1705

The average term of office of these viceroys was seven and a half years. During the reign of Monclova, the first of the Bourbon kings ascended the throne of Spain, and the Peruvian viceroys of the eighteenth century were the appointees of the Spanish Bourbons. They were thirteen in number, and the average duration of their terms of office was essentially the same as that of the viceroys of the seventeenth century. They were:

The Marquis de Castel dos Rios .	1705–1710
Diego Ladron de Guevara . . .	1710–1716
Carmine Nicolas Carraccioli,	
Prince of Santo Bono . . .	1716–1720
Morcillo Rubio de Auñon . . .	1720–1724
Jose de Armendariz,	
Marquis of Castelfuerte . .	1724–1736
The Marquis of Villagarcia . .	1736–1745

Jose Antonio Manso,
    Count of Superunda .   .   . 1745–1761
Manuel de Amat   .   .   .   1761–1776
Manuel de Guirion   .   .   . 1776–1780
Augustin de Jaurequi 1780–1784
Teodoro de Croix   1784–1790
Francisco Gil de Toboada y Lemos . 1790–1796
Ambrosio O'Higgins,
    Marquis of Osorno   .   .   . 1796–1801

Until the establishment of the viceroyalties of New Granada and Buenos Aires, the jurisdiction of the viceroy of Peru was coextensive with the Spanish possessions in South America; for the several captains-general were subject to the superior authority of the Peruvian viceroy.

CHAPTER VI

THE CONQUEST OF CHILE

WHEN Chile first became known to the Spaniards, her inhabitants had advanced beyond the earliest phases of society; they were no longer hunters or merely shepherds; they had adopted a settled life and lived by agriculture. They cultivated a great variety of plants, and in some parts of the country had developed extensive means of irrigation. They had learned to cook their food, and from grains and fruits to prepare various kinds of spirituous liquors.[1]

Their fundamental social organization was a village, or hamlet, at the head of which stood a chief called an *ulmen*. The several members of the village held their lands as private prop-

[1] On this period of Chilian history, one may find ample material for a general view in Barros Arana, *Historia generale de Chile ;* Gay, *Historia física y política de Chile ;* Mackenna, *Historia crítica y social de la Ciudad de Santiago ;* and Molina, *The Geographical, Natural, and Civil History of Chile.*

erty, and transmitted them to their children as
an inheritance.

The spoils of Peru stimulated the adventurers who had taken possession of that country
to make other conquests. In 1535 Almagro led five hundred and seventy Spaniards
and fifteen thousand Peruvians into Chile.
Taking the route over the mountains, instead
of that along the shore, one hundred and fifty
Spaniards and ten thousand Peruvians perished
on the way. The hostility with which Almagro was received in Chile persuaded him to
withdraw, and he returned to Peru in 1538,
where he took possession of the ancient capital, Cuzco. This brought him into war with
the brother of Pizarro, in which he was killed
and his army scattered.

The death of Almagro left Francisco Pizarro
master of the Spanish possessions of South
America, with a prospect of further conquests
in Chile. In spite of the arrival of Pedro San-
chez de Hoz and Carmargo, commissioned by
the court of Spain to conquer Chile, Pizarro
sent Pedro de Valdivia to take possession of
that country. De Hoz, who participated in
the expedition, was beheaded there in 1546.
The expedition of Valdivia was undertaken
with the intention of establishing a permanent
settlement ; and to this end the leader was provided not only with soldiers, but with every-

thing necessary to the formation of a colony. On the 24th of February, 1541, Valdivia laid the foundation of the future capital of Chile, and called it Santiago. It was laid out after the plan which had been adopted as a general guide in the establishment of Spanish-American cities. Towards the end of the eighteenth century, in 1787, Santiago contained more than forty thousand inhabitants, and the number was then rapidly increasing.

After establishing Santiago, Valdivia founded other cities, of which Concepcion, Imperial, and Valdivia were instances, the last named being the first city founded in America which took its name from one of the Spanish conquerors. In this matter the Spanish stand in marked contrast with the British settlers, who took occasion in naming their towns to commemorate their heroes. It was under Valdivia that Francisco de Aguirre was dispatched with two hundred men to make conquests east of the Andes. As a result of these conquests, the provinces of Cujo and Tucuman became a part of the dominions of Chile.

When Valdivia was in Chile, he introduced a form of feudalism similar to that which had been established in Mexico and Peru. As a reward for his efforts in the conquest and settlement of the country, Valdivia looked for some special recognition by the king. He sent

an agent to Spain with a large sum of money,
and " commissioned him to use his utmost ex-
ertions to obtain for him the perpetual government of the conquered country, with the title
of Marquis of Arauco." [1] While Valdivia was
seeking honors for his past achievements, the
Indians were preparing a revolt which was
destined to lead to his ruin. His army was
defeated, and he was made a prisoner and put
to death.

On the death of Valdivia, his agent, Alderete,
who had been sent to Spain, was appointed to
take charge of the government of Chile, and
carry on the conquest of that region. He was
furnished by Philip II. with six hundred soldiers, but all of these, except three or four,
were lost by the burning of the ship near Porto
Bello. Alderete himself escaped, but died not
long afterwards on the island of Taboga, in the
gulf of Panama.[2] After the news of the unfortunate outcome of Alderete's undertaking
had reached Peru, the viceroy appointed his
son, Don Garcia Hurtado de Mendoza, governor of Chile. The persistent hostility of the
Araucanians made it necessary for the governor to be supported by a large military force.
Throughout the viceroy's dominions there were
not wanting adventurers whose expectations
had not been realized. The call for soldiers

[1] Molina, ii., 122.   [2] *Ibid.*, 147.

issued by the viceroy offered them at least occupation and a new field for exploits. Led by
various motives, they presented themselves for
service in sufficient numbers to constitute an
important army. Ten ships under Don Garcia
in person took the infantry to the coast of
Chile, while the cavalry went by land under
the quartermaster - general, Garcia Ramon.
The infantry landed near Concepcion in April,
1557, but the cavalry did not arrive till some
months later. The Araucanians were not ter-
rified by the great show of force made by the
Spaniards, and determined to adhere to their
ancient policy of war. The barbarous practices
of the governor in either mutilating or putting
to death all persons taken in war, had not the
effect to subdue the enemy, but rather to in-
flame them with a desire for revenge. Even
the women were moved by this spirit, and
fought in the ranks with the men. But all
their bravery did not permanently avail against
the more effective arms of the Spaniards.

The conquest of Cujo which had been begun
by Francisco de Aguirre was later completed by
Pedro Castillo, acting under the orders of Governor Mendoza. Castillo founded two cities
east of the Andes, which he called San Juan
and Mendoza. The latter was named in honor
of the family of Governor Mendoza.

Mendoza's troubled reign as governor of

Chile came to an end on the return of Francisco Villagran from Spain as his successor. Mendoza returned to Lima, and was appointed viceroy of the kingdom of Peru. The first important object of Villagran's activity was to restore the province of Tucuman to Chile. In this enterprise Villagran was successful, but Tucuman remained only a short time under the dominion of Chile, for before the end of the sixteenth century the Spanish court caused it to be reannexed to Peru.

When Villagran became governor of Chile, he believed that the power of the Araucanians had been broken; but neither he nor his predecessors properly appreciated the character of this remarkable people, whom they fancied they had overthrown. Molina calls the Araucanian the " invincible," and says " he cannot be made to submit to the bitterest reverses of fortune. His losses themselves, so far from dejecting or dismaying him, appear to inspire him with more strength and valor." [1] Villagran died, leaving his eldest son Pedro to succeed him, and yet the Araucanian was not subdued.

The spirit of the Araucanians is expressed in the reply which the Araucanian ambassador is said to have made to the governor of Chile in the last decade of the sixteenth century. The

[1] *History of Chile*, ii., 176.

governor had endeavored to impress the ambassador with an idea of the great power of the king of Spain, and to make evident the necessity of submission on the part of the Araucanians.

"We are not ignorant," the ambassador replied, "of the power of your prince, which extends from the east to the west.   But we are not to be despised, for although we are but a small people, we have nevertheless hitherto resisted his immense power. Your ideas respecting peace are very different from ours.   By peace we understand an entire cessation of hostilities, which is to be followed by a complete renunciation on your part of any pretended right of control over us, and the restoration of all those lands which you have occupied in our territories. You, on the contrary, under that name, seek to subject us, to which we will never consent while we have a drop of blood left in our veins." [1]

This speech may have no more authenticity than many other speeches reported by historians; but that it represents the spirit of the Araucanians is sufficiently indicated by the events of their long struggle with the Spaniards.

From year to year the war with the Araucanians continued without the prospect of a near end; and it was evident that while it lasted there was little hope of bringing the Indians to

[1] Molina, ii., 215.

adopt the Christian faith. Louis Valdivia, a Jesuit, went to Spain in the early part of the seventeenth century, and presented this aspect of the case to the king, Philip III. Wishing to remove all obstacles to the conversion of the Indians, the king proposed that the river Bio-bio should be the boundary between the Spanish and the Araucanians, and that the war should be terminated by a permanent peace. But this plan could not be carried out. There were enough persons interested in having the war continue to defeat the peace policy.

After about thirty years of almost uninterrupted war with the Araucanians, there was still no prospect of permanent peace, and the difficulty of controlling and protecting the Chilian settlements from Lima became apparent. In order to remedy this defect and furnish an authority for the government of Chile independent of the audiencia of Peru, Philip II. was finally moved to set up the royal audiencia of Chile. This body was composed of four judges and a fiscal. It took up its residence in Concepcion, in August, 1567, and under its authority Ruiz Gamboa was placed in command of the army.

The rule of the audiencia had many of the weaknesses of a government by a council. These were specially conspicuous here, in the presence of a determined and unsubdued enemy.

In 1568, therefore, in order to avoid these evils, and to give greater concentration of authority, Don Melchor de Bravo was made president of the audiencia, civil governor, and military commander, with extensive powers in each department. This order of things, however, did not last long, for in 1575 a special commissioner arrived from the court of Spain, empowered to reorganize the government. On his advice the audiencia was dissolved, on grounds of economy, and the members ordered to return to Peru. Philip II. then appointed Rodrigo Quiroga to the office of governor.

Quiroga died in 1580, and when his death had become known in Spain, Don Alonso Sotomayor was appointed to succeed him. On the way to Chile, Sotomayor landed at Buenos Aires with a troop of six hundred men, in 1583, and proceeded across the continent to Santiago. During all the governmental changes through which Chile passed at this time, the barbarous war with the Araucanians continued with such equal fortune as to put off indefinitely the day of final victory.

When Garcia Ramon became governor and at the same time captain-general of Chile, he received a thousand soldiers from Europe and two hundred and fifty from Mexico, which raised the number of regular troops under his command to three thousand. This army he

directed against the Araucanians, but in a
short time it was completely overthrown, and
the soldiers, almost without exception, were
either killed or taken prisoners, or scattered.
This disaster led the court of Spain to make
special provision for defending the frontier.
In 1608, orders were issued that a force of two
thousand men should be maintained to protect
the Spanish settlement against the Araucanians, and for their support 292,279 dollars were
annually appropriated from the treasury of Peru.

During the administration of Garcia Ramon,
in September, 1609, the audiencia, which had
been suppressed thirty-four years before, was
re-established. The residence of the audiencia
was fixed at Santiago, and Ramon now enjoyed
the title of president of the audiencia in addition to those of governor and captain-general.
But he died about a year later, and in accordance with a decree passed at the time of the
re-establishment of the audencia, the oldest
judge, Don Louis Merlo de la Fuente, succeeded to the presidency, and assumed the
control of the government.

The Araucanian war was finally ended after
almost a century's duration. On the part of
the Spaniards, this was accomplished by Don
Francisco Zuñiga, Marquis de Baydes, who
arrived in Chile as governor in 1640. The
treaty of peace was concluded and ratified early

in the following year.   As a result of this treaty
prisoners were released, commerce was established between the two peoples, deserted lands
were repopulated, and the missionaries began
their efforts to convert the Indians.   In view
of this treaty the fear was entertained on the
part of the Araucanians that the Spaniards designed to make them unused to arms with the
view of ultimately conquering them ; while the
Spaniards feared that in peace the Araucanians
would increase in numbers and finally become
masters of the whole country.   The Biobio
was made the line of division between the territories of the Araucanians and the Spaniards.
The Araucanians recognized the king of Spain
as the feudal superior, and the Spanish troops
withdrew from the forts of the Indians' territory.   The peace lasted fifteen years, when it
was interrupted by the Araucanians, under the
pretext that the Spaniards had encroached
upon their territory.   Hereafter hostile relations were maintained till 1724, when a new
peace was formed, which was observed till
1766.   But mutual suspicion and the natural
antagonism of different races made it difficult to obtain a permanent peace.   Yet, in
1780, there was formed at Santiago a treaty,
in obedience to which the Araucanians were
maintained in a state of tranquillity during the
rest of the colonial period.   Under this treaty

they maintained a representative at Santiago, commissioned to watch over their interests, and to cause their rights to be recognized and respected by the captain-general.

In the first half of the eighteenth century, under the rule of Gonzaga, an attempt was made to have the Araucanians live in cities. When informed of this project, the national council of the Araucanians resolved, in the first place,

"to delay as long as possible the business, by equivocal replies and delusive promises ; then, when pressed to commence building, to require from the Spaniards tools and other necessary aid ; to have recourse to arms whenever they found themselves obliged to begin the work, but to act in such a manner that only the provinces that were compelled to build should declare war, the others remaining neutral in order to be able to mediate a peace ; to come to a general rupture whenever they found that the mediation of the latter would not be accepted ; to allow the missionaries to depart without injury, as they had nothing to accuse them with but of being Spaniards ; and to choose immediately a Toqui, who should attend to the execution of these regulations, and to have everything in readiness to take the field as soon as circumstances should require it."[1]

In the eighteenth century the governor, or

[1] Molina, ii., 258.

captain-general, of Chile acquired a new importance, in that it became to a certain extent
customary for the holder of this office to be
promoted to some more desirable post, often
to the position of viceroy of Peru. Next to
this chief officer in importance stood the royal
audiencia. As a tribunal, this body, through
its two branches, exercised civil and criminal
jurisdiction. Its judgments were final, except
in cases involving more than ten thousand
dollars. These might be appealed to the
Council of the Indies. Other important courts
were the court of finance, of the *crusada*, of
vacant lands, and the tribunal of commerce.

The kingdom of Chile was divided into thirteen provinces, which were governed by officers
known at different times as corregidors, pre-
fects, and sub-delegates. The original intention of the law appears to have been that they
should be appointed by the king, but the great
distance of this region from the Spanish court
made it inconvenient to carry out this intention,
and it became customary for the captain-general
to appoint them. Like their superior, the
captain-general, they exercised both civil and
military functions. They served without other
pay than the fees of their office. It was designed that the capital of each province should
have a municipal organization, called a *cabildo*,
composed of two alcaldes, a high sheriff, a

judge, a procurator, and a council of regidores. The alcaldes were chosen annually by the *cabildo*, and had jurisdiction in the first instance in both civil and criminal cases. In judicial affairs, their powers were not greatly unlike those of a justice of the peace.

The military force of the country consisted of the regular troops, the militia, and certain companies of dragoons supported by the municipality of Santiago. In the last decade of the eighteenth century the veteran troops of Chile numbered one thousand nine hundred and seventy-six men. At the same time there were nearly sixteen thousand men enrolled in the militia. The companies of city militia served as aids to the police, guarding prisons and escorting criminals, but by their militia service they were not exempt from the duties of the ordinary military service.

After the destruction of Concepcion by an earthquake, the city of Imperial became the capital of a bishopric, in 1570. The territory embraced in this diocese was the southern portion of Chile, extending as far north as the river Maule. But in the last decade of the eighteenth century, there were two dioceses in Chile, the one having its centre at Santiago, the other at Concepcion. One comprised that part of Chile extending from the southern border of Peru to the river Maule, and also the province of Cuyo.   The other diocese embraced that part of Chile south of the river Maule.   The power of the Inquisition was also felt in Chile before the end of the colonial period.   It rested on a firm basis at Lima, and had established a commissioner and several subordinates at Santiago.   The late development of this part of South America is indicated by the fact that prior to the outbreak of the revolution, there was no printing-press in Chile. The first one established there was in 1812. In February of this year, *La Aurora de Chile* began to be published.   This was long after the introduction of printing into Mexico, Peru, and Buenos Aires.

CHAPTER VII

VENEZUELA AND COLOMBIA

IN the early years of Spanish dominion, the northern part of South America was within the limits of the jurisdiction of the audiencia of San Domingo, while the territory of Ecuador was under the immediate control of the audiencia of Quito, which recognized the viceroy of Peru as its superior. The audiencia of San Domingo might and did interfere in conflicts between the Indians and the settlers, and to this end employed a commissioner to mediate in the affairs of the contending parties. In 1527, John Ampues was sent on a mission of this sort to the region now occupied by Venezuela, and was accompanied by sixty men. He founded the city of Coro, under the name of Santa Ana de Coro, which became the seat of the government of this region, and maintained this distinction until 1576, when Caracas was made the capital.

The wars in which Charles V. was engaged,
and the ordinary undertakings of his government involved him in expenses which exceeded
his regular revenues; and to supply the deficit
he had recourse to borrowing. Conspicuous
among his creditors were the merchants of
Augsburg, especially the commercial house of
Welser. These merchants demanded of the
emperor in consideration of loans already
made, and of others which it was expected he
would require, that the province of Venezuela
should be granted to them as an hereditary fief
of the crown. The province as granted embraced the coast from Cape de la Vela to
Maracapana, and extended indefinitely into the
interior. The principal conditions of the grant
were: (1) That the Welsers, within two years,
should found two cities and three forts; (2)
that they should arm four ships for the transportation of three hundred Spaniards and fifty
master-miners who should be employed in
working the mines for the benefit of the company; (3) that the emperor should grant the
title of *adelantado* to the person whom the
Welsers should nominate; (4) that the emperor
should allow the Welsers to receive four per
cent. of the king's fifth of the product of the
mines, and another portion of land twelve
leagues square, which they might choose in
any part of the conquered country; (5) that

the company should have power to make slaves of the Indians who should refuse to submit without force. These provisions were not carried out, except in so far as their execution would be advantageous to the Germans. The sixth provision was so construed as to warrant the settlers in reducing to slavery all Indians that fell into their hands.

"The execution of this fatal treaty was committed to Ambrose Alfinger, whom the company nominated governor of their new territory. Another German, named Sallier, was appointed his lieutenant. Four hundred adventurers formed the body of the expedition, who left Europe in 1528, and arrived the same year at Coro. The government was willingly resigned by John Ampues in favor of Alfinger, who soon informed himself of the resources which the country presented for the gratification of avarice. He expected to find there mines of gold more abundant than those of Cibao and Mexico, whose renown at that time resounded all over Europe. But when he learned that there was no mine wrought there; that the Indians formed but small scattered settlements, and were totally unacquainted with every sort of luxury; that gold there was not manufactured into coin; and that the only use made of some particles of that metal which the inundations of the rivers conveyed, or chance presented upon the surface of the earth, was limited to some trinkets, without any

other artificial preparation than what they received
in moulds coarsely made : when he observed, in
short, that the means of accumulating riches were
not so easy there as he had imagined, he adopted
the pernicious plan of penetrating with an armed
force into the interior of the country, in order to
commit depredations on the inhabitants, and dispose for money of all the prisoners he could take." [1]

For eighteen years the Welsers continued to
ravage this unfortunate country.   Alfinger was
killed by the Indians in 1531, when the control
of the undertaking fell into the hands of his
lieutenant.   But in 1533 George Spira was
sent to be the governor of the colony.   He
took with him four hundred men from Spain
and the Canary Islands.   With these he continued the policy of his predecessor, and for
five years he scoured the wilderness for gold
and slaves.   In 1539 he returned to Coro with
only eighty of the four hundred men with whom
he had set out.   The next year, 1540, Spira
died on the return voyage from San Domingo,
and the headship of the colony was conferred
upon the bishop of Coro, Rodrigo de Bastides. [2]
The bishop had been four years in the country,
and there is no evidence that he had protested

[1] Depons, i., 24.

[2] Caracas became later the ecclesiastical capital of the country, and Bastides was counted as the first of the bishops.   For
a complete list of the bishops of Caracas, see Restrepo, *Historia de la Revolucion de la Republica de Colombia*, i., 595.

against the abominable practices of Spira. He had not only been silent, but, having succeeded to the place of chief authority, he even followed the example of his predecessors. He sent an expedition against the Indians of Maracaibo, which returned a small amount of gold and five hundred Indian slaves. Another expedition sought El Dorado, but the gilded prince was not found, and a few more outrages were added to those which marked the rule of this company. Almost the only effort in behalf of civilization during the eighteen years of the Welsers' domination was the founding of the city of Tocuyo, in 1545, by Governor Caravajal. Its first population was fifty-nine Spaniards; its government was placed in the hands of two alcaldes and four regidores. This was the only municipal establishment made in Venezuela under the German company.

In 1545, Charles V. rescinded the grant which had been made to the Germans, and the province of Venezuela reverted to the crown. It was then placed under a governor sent from Spain. The effect of this change was to diminish plundering expeditions, and to increase the security of property. Under the new order of things, the Indians, instead of being captured and sold as slaves, were distributed among the Spanish settlers under the law of *encomiendas*.

The first of the governors who directed the affairs of Venezuela after the province was brought immediately under the king was Juan Perez de Tolosa, who died in 1548. During the second half of the sixteenth century the history of Venezuela is made up of accounts of exploring expeditions, of the founding of towns, and of wars with the Indians. It was not until near the close of the seventeenth century that the conquest was complete; but in the meantime the country suffered under repeated attacks of freebooters and pirates.

In the early part of the eighteenth century, the trade between Venezuela and Spain passed into the hands of the Compañia Guipuzcoana. This company was composed of a number of Biscayan merchants, who offered to put an end to the contraband trade with Venezuela, on condition of receiving the monopoly of trade with that province. Under the original form of the grant the company was permitted to send annually two vessels of forty or fifty guns, carrying products of Spain to the port of La Guayra, and was charged to seize all vessels engaged in the contraband trade. In 1734 the privileges of the company were enlarged; it might send any number of vessels desired, and dispatch them from the ports of San Sebastian and Los Pasages as well as from Cadiz. The spoils of the contraband vessels captured were

divided between the crew and the company, so
that the former might get one third, and the
latter two thirds. The law prohibiting trade
between the colonies was so far suspended in
favor of the company that it might send to
Vera Cruz the cacao which it was not able to
ship to Spain. All cases concerning this trade
requiring a judicial decision might be referred
to the governor of Caracas, and from his decision an appeal might be taken to the Council
of the Indies. Although the company enjoyed
a practical monopoly of this trade, yet the king
might create a rival, by granting similar privileges to others in case the company already
established did not bring him the desired advantages. The liability of being obliged to
carry on this trade in competition with another
company made the existing company careful to
meet the expectations of the king. In the
course of time, however, the possibility of
rivalry was in a measure removed. By the
decree of 1742, the privilege of exclusive commerce with at least a part of the territory was
granted, and ten years later the region of its
exclusive control was enlarged. This naturally
excited the fears of the inhabitants, and for a
long time the company encountered opposition
from the side of the people. The fact that
the privilege of exclusive trade had been sought
and obtained by the company was all that was

necessary to awaken these fears and arouse discontent on the part of the inhabitants. This
discontent was, however, in some measure
abated by the agreement reached in 1750, to
form an assembly composed of members of the
company and planters in equal numbers, in
which the governor-general of the province of
Venezuela should preside, and which should
fix the price to be paid by the company for
cacao. In case some of the inhabitants were
not satisfied with the price thus established,
they might send a sixth part of their cacao to
Spain on their own account in vessels belonging to the company. Apparently to avoid
extortion, the company was required to submit for approval to the superior governmental
authority of the province a schedule of the
prices at which it was proposed to sell the
wares brought from Europe.

The success of the company depended on its
being able to stop the operations of foreign
traders and to transfer to itself the trade which
they had carried on. This involved it in an
annual expense of two hundred thousand dollars, in supporting ten vessels, containing
eighty-six guns and five hundred and eighteen
men. At the ports participating in this trade
warehouses were constructed, and wharves and
other facilities for landing and loading goods
were provided. And this activity of the com-

pany contributed to the development of the
country, as seen in the increase in the number
of towns and in the extension of the area of
planting.   Six vessels of at least three hundred
tons each were sent annually by the company
to the province, and to the previously existing
trade in cacao was added a trade in hides and
tobacco, and through this increase in the business of the province the duties became adequate
to cover the expenses of the government, a
state of things which had not existed for two
centuries.   " In short, everything in the province of Venezuela assumed a cheerful aspect,
an air of prosperity not seen in any other
Spanish possession." [1]

In the course of time the company yielded
to the temptation to corrupt the assembly that
had power to fix the prices of the articles involved in its trade.   In alliance with the Dutch
of Curaçoa, it took part in the contraband
trade, and by depriving the mother country of
its proper duties, it added to the evils which it
had promised to abolish.   But the inhabitants
of the province, as well as the company, found
an advantage in the unlawful trade, and it became increasingly difficult to prevent it.   Spain
was obliged to acknowledge that here as well as
in other parts of her American possessions the
restrictive system had failed, and Venezuela,

[1] Depons, ii. 18.

during the last quarter of the eighteenth century, shared with the other provinces of Spanish America in the advantages of freedom established by the decree of 1778. The object in discriminating between the large and the smaller ports, and in making a lower rate of duties for the smaller ports, was to encourage trade with them, which might not otherwise prove to be profitable.[1] The major ports of the captaincy-general of Caracas were La Guayra, Porto Cavello, and Maracaibo, while Cumana, Barcelona, Margareta, and Guiana were the minor ports. If, after landing, goods were transported from a major to a minor port, the difference between the two rates of duties was refunded to the shipper; but, on the other hand, if goods were carried from a minor to a major port, this difference had to be added to the duty already paid.

Under the monopoly of this company, there was an important revival of the commerce and agriculture of the colony. The number of articles cultivated for commerce was increased, but the control of the monopoly became oppressive. Yet in spite of the popular opposition, which in 1749 nearly plunged the country into civil war, the company retained its privileges till 1778. It was succeeded by the Compañia Filipinas, which lasted, however, only till 1780.

[1] Depons, ii., 22.

During the later years of Spain's domination in Venezuela, the king was represented in the government of the province by a captain-general, whose position and powers with respect to public affairs were not greatly unlike those of the viceroy. He was president of the audiencia; he was at the head of the military establishment; and as the highest officer of the province he was charged with its internal administration and foreign relations. He might report to the Council of the Indies in criticism of the action of the audiencia, and "even direct secret inquiries against any member" of this body suspected of illegal conduct. In cases where the law failed to specify the required action, the captain-general might take such measures as seemed to be demanded by the public welfare. But in this field he was restrained by the consideration of the trial that might follow the close of his term of service. In addition to his administrative and judicial powers, he might appoint various subordinate officers, and fill provisionally certain vacancies which could be filled permanently only by the king.

The term for which the captain-general was appointed was seven years, and the amount of his annual salary was nine thousand dollars. The perquisites of his office and the sums received in his capacity as judge amounted to as

much as his specified salary.   It was apparently
the intention of the makers of the law under
which he held office, to cause him to stand
apart from the people he governed.   He might
not engage in business, or enter into close social
relations with his subjects.   But, like other
officers, at the close of his term of office he
was subject to the trial known as *residencia*.
For a period of seventy days citizens of all
classes had an opportunity to bring before
a properly commissioned judge complaints
against the captain-general concerning any
abuse of authority of which he was thought to
be guilty.   If any charge was made, the judge
took the succeeding period of seventy days to
examine and render a decision in the case.
The case with the decision rendered was then
passed on to be finally determined by the
Council of the Indies.   In 1799, trials of this
kind, to which all the authorities of the Indies
had previously been liable, were confined to
the viceroys, captains-general, presidents, political and military governors, intendants, and
corregidors.[1]

Until 1718 this province remained within the
jurisdiction of the audiencia of San Domingo,
when it passed under the authority of the
audiencia of Santa Fé.   But a few years later
it was transferred to its original superior, and

[1] Baralt and Diaz, *Historia de Venezuela*, i., 306.

in 1786 it was brought under the new audiencia of Caracas, whose jurisdiction had the same territorial extent as that of the captain-general, and embraced the districts of Venezuela, Maracaibo, Cumana, Varinas, Guiana, and the island of Margareta. In addition to the secular courts, there were other tribunals that took cognizance of ecclesiastical affairs exclusively.

At the head of the financial administration of the captaincy-general stood the intendant, whose authority extended over the whole territory subject to the captain-general. In conducting the affairs of his office, he was assisted by the governors of the several districts, who acted as his deputies. In the constitution of his office he was given a large measure of independence. He might impose any regulation which appeared to him expedient in the financial management of his province. All payments from the treasury had to be ordered by him. He might fill provisionally any vacancy which occurred in the administration. The legal term of his office was five years, and his annual salary was nine thousand dollars, with fees amounting to as much more.

The consulate, a tribunal for the adjudication of cases involving commercial affairs, was one of the most important institutions of the later years of the colonial dependence. It was established in various parts of Spanish America, but established at Caracas by a decree of June 3, 1793. It was formed after the model of the consulate of Seville. It was composed of the intendant, who was the president, a prior, two consuls, nine counsellors, and a syndic, together with their deputies. These members held office usually for two years, one half of them being renewed by an election held on the 5th of January of each year. Besides these, there were five permanent members, namely, an assessor, a secretary, a registrar, and two porters. All white persons of reputable lives, except ecclesiastics, were eligible to membership. At first the annual salaries ranged from $160 to $800. The prior received $600, a consul $400, the syndic $300, the secretary $800, with $300 for a clerk, the assessor $500, the registrar $400, and each porter $180. By a decree of January 12, 1796, these salaries were increased so that a prior received $1600, a consul $1400, a syndic 1200, a secretary $1400, with an allowance for a clerk, an assessor $1500, a registrar $1000, with $300 for a clerk, and each porter $300.

The revenues of the consulate were derived from fines and from a duty imposed on imports and exports. This duty, taking all articles into consideration, amounted to about one per cent. on commodities imported from or exported to Europe or other parts of Spanish

America; and three per cent. on commodities imported from or exported to foreign colonies. There were certain exceptions to this method of reckoning, as when mules and horses paid a dollar a head without regard to their value.

In its jurisdiction and form of procedure the consulate of Caracas followed the essential provisions of the laws under which consulates were established in Mexico, Peru, and other parts of Spanish America.[1] "All disputes which arise between the merchants or retail dealers and their associates and deputies, on matters relating to commerce, such as purchases, sales, exchanges, assurances, partnership - accounts, freight of vessels — in a word, on everything recognized by the consulate of Bilbao," were clearly within the jurisdiction of the consulate of Caracas; and by a decree of July, 1795, it was given cognizance of " all causes relating to damages, or bargains contracted between the captains of merchant vessels, and merchants interested in their freight and cargoes." [2] Although the territorial jurisdiction of the consulate of Caracas was coextensive with the jurisdiction of the captain-general, yet for the greater convenience of the parties concerned deputies were appointed for the ports of Maracaibo, Coro, Porto Cabello, Cumana, La

[1] *Recopilacion de las Indias*, Libro ix., Titulo 36.
[2] Depons, ii., 77, 78.

Guayra, and Margareta, who were empowered
to try all cases that might legitimately come
before the consulate.   The deputy in each
port might nominate two persons to assist him.
From decisions rendered by the deputies, as
from decisions by the ordinary tribunal, an appeal might be taken to the *alzadas*, a court of
appeal composed of the intendant and two
judges nominated by him.   The decision of
the consulate was final for cases involving eight
hundred dollars or less, but cases involving
much smaller sums might be appealed from
the deputy's court.   In Cumana, Porto Cabello,
and Maracaibo a case of more than two hundred dollars; in Guiana and Coro a case of
more than one hundred dollars; and in the
island of Margareta a case of more than fifty
dollars might be appealed.   An appeal might
also be taken from the deputy to the consulate.
If the consulate confirmed the deputy's decision
there was no further appeal; but if the deputy's
decision was modified a further appeal to the
alzadas was permitted.

In addition to its activity as a court of justice, the consulate was expected to take the
initiative in certain matters of administration
not concerned with the judiciary.   In this
capacity, it was required that the prior, the
two consuls, their assistants, the syndic, and
their respective deputies, the secretary, the

paymaster, and the treasurer should assemble twice a month, and any officer absent from the assembly was liable to a fine of twenty dollars. The assembly was permitted to correspond directly with the king, and was required to suggest to him such measures as might further the development of the agriculture, industry, and commerce of the province. Through its power to encourage the making of good roads, to cause the harbor of La Guayra to be improved, and to help render navigable such rivers as might serve for the transportation of produce, it was in a position, with enlightened activity, to advance the material prosperity of the province. But zeal was wanting, the opportunity was neglected, and the expectations of beneficent achievements were not realized. There is no evidence of improvement under its influence. On the other hand, in the last decade of the eighteenth century, the exportations show a marked decline. Comparing the period of four years, from 1792 to 1796, with the following four years, from 1796 to 1800, the extent of this decline becomes manifest. The value of the exports of cacao, indigo, cotton, and coffee in the first period was 12,252,415 dollars; the value of the same articles exported in the second period was 6,442,318 dollars, showing a diminution of 5,810,097 dollars. Making all due allowance for the effect of the European

12

war, there will remain still some portion of the diminution to be attributed to the carelessness and inefficiency of the consulate.

Another side of the social development of Venezuela was seen in the establishment of schools. The first provision for education was made by the bishop of Caracas, in 1696. He founded a college for ecclesiastics, which, in 1724, was, by royal charter, transformed into a university. Prior to this, young men wishing a secular education were obliged to visit the universities of San Domingo, Mexico, or Bogotá, or resort to the schools of Europe. The seminary of Merida desired a similar extension, but the king of Spain, Charles IV., refused to confer upon this institution the charter of a university, " because His Majesty did not think it proper that education should become general in America." [1] As to the education of women, it is reported that " for fear of illicit correspondence few of them were taught even to write." With the limited opportunities for education which the colony afforded, there was little demand for the products of the printing-press, which was not set up here till the beginning of the nineteenth century, and even then was subject to severe censorship. The population of Venezuela at that time was about 800,000. Of these there were 12,000 whites

[1] See Baralt and Diaz, *Historia de Venezuela*, i., 414.

born in Europe, 200,000 creoles, 406,000 of mixed blood, 62,000 negro slaves, and 120,000 Indians.

If we turn to the other portion of this northern region of South America, to the territory of New Granada, which for a time was in political union with Venezuela, we shall find that the most conspicuous events in the early history of this district were the discoveries and settlements on the Isthmus, the expedition up the Magdalena River to Bogotá under the command of Gonzalo Jimenez Quesada, and the two expeditions to this point from Peru and Venezuela. Belalcazar, who had come from Peru, and Federmann, who had been sent by Governor Spira, of Venezuela, yielded their rights of conquest in favor of Quesada, who had reached Bogotá in April, 1537. The three forces were united, and the leaders determined together to carry the news of their discoveries to Spain. In memory of his native country, Quesada called this region the New Kingdom of Granada, and on the 6th of August, 1538, with solemn ceremony, he established Santa Fé de Bogotá as its capital, to which Charles V. two years later accorded the title of city. In 1548, the emperor granted to Bogotá a coat-of-arms and a standard, and in 1565 its title as the " very noble and very loyal city " was confirmed by Philip II. Under the stimulus of reports of fertile lands and great wealth, many colonists found their way into this region carrying with them such seeds and domestic animals as would enable them to maintain an independent existence and develop the resources of the country. Here, as in other parts of America, the eagerness of the Spaniards to acquire wealth made them careless of the welfare of the Indians, who, under the cruel treatment to which they were subjected, rapidly disappeared. And the spoils which were the fruit of this oppression were even more abundant than the treasure of Atahualpa.[1] Not only was the property of the natives taken, and their lands distributed among the invaders, but the natives themselves were also reduced to the position of serfs. This assignment of lands and Indians to the Spanish settlers and the formation of a municipal council were the essential features of founding a municipality; and it was in this way that Panama, Santa Marta, Cartagena, Cali, Bogotá, and afterwards other cities were established.

Of the three leaders who visited Spain to announce the discovery and settlement of this country, Federmann did not return, but went to Flanders to offer his services to the crown; Belalcazar was granted Popayan and the province of Antioquia. Quesada was given the

[1] Pereira, *Les États-Unis de Colombie*, 7.

title of marshal and appointed a regidor of the municipality of Bogotá with an income of three thousand ducats.

The first attempt to remove the inconveniences caused by the lack of a general and stable government was the establishment of a royal audiencia at Bogotá, in 1550; but this was not eminently successful on account of the abuses instituted or tolerated by the members. Fourteen years later the colony was converted into a presidency, and Andres Venero de Leyva was made the first president. Leyva's wisdom and activity contributed much to the well-being of his subjects. He established schools, decreed rules and ordinances for the good government of the cities, caused roads and bridges to be constructed, encouraged the raising of mules, as a means of facilitating transportation, introduced coinage, prohibiting payments in gold dust, and obliged the *encomenderos* to live where they held their lands and serfs, in order that they might " fulfil the duties which the law imposed upon them with respect to the Indians, instead of abandoning them to the brutality of the mayor domos." Leyva governed the colony from 1564 to 1575, and during the following one hundred and sixty-five years a long series of governors came and went without producing any important change in the character of the administration. The population felt the hampering force of Spain's restrictive system, and advanced very slowly in civilization. The inhabitants in the interior, about Bogotá, suffered not only from Spanish legislation, but also from their geographical isolation, while the towns on the coast were impeded in their development by a constant fear of pirates, and by the frequent plundering expeditions to which they were subjected.

In 1718 the presidency was transformed into a viceroyalty, but the government remained in this form only four years, and was then reduced again to its former rank. The viceroyalty was, however, finally re-established in 1739, and in it was included not only the territory of New Granada, but also the presidency of Quito. At the same time the audiencias of Panama and Quito were abolished, and political authority was centralized in the viceroy and audiencia of Bogotá. The viceroyalty, under the title of the New Kingdom of Granada, embraced the provinces of Tierra Firme, Cartagena, Santa Marta and Riohacha, Antioquia, Pamplona and Socorro, Tunja, Santa Fé, Neiva and Mariquira, Popayan and Pasto, together with Maracaibo, Caracas, Cumana, and La Guayana, the territory of the later republic of Venezuela, and Quito, Cuenca, and Guayaquil, territory later embraced in the republic of Ecuador. The administration of the first vice-

roy, Don Sebastian de Eslaba, was marked by
the noteworthy and unsuccessful attack of Admiral Vernon, who first took Porto Bello, and
then directed his forces against the city of
Cartagena. The English force in this attack
comprised 28 vessels of the line, 12 frigates, and
130 transports, carrying 9000 soldiers, 2000
macheteros from Jamaica, and 15,000 marines.
Against this attacking force the viceroy was
able to bring only about 3000 men, of whom
only 1100 were regulars. Yet the achievements of the English were not in keeping with
their great preparations. They had evidently
planned to assume a position of permanent advantage in this region, yet they were obliged
to retire with the loss of about one half
of their force, and with their purpose unat-
tained.[1] This successful resistance on the part
of the Spanish left the viceroy's government
free for a number of years to carry out internal
improvements, to construct roads, bridges, and
aqueducts, to introduce a better financial organization of the colonies, to develop manufactures of tobacco and powder, and, with the
books left by the Jesuits on their expulsion, to
establish a public library. A few years later,
however, the internal peace was disturbed by
an uprising of the Indians, whose principal

[1] Restrepo, *Historia de la Revolucion de la Republica de
Colombia*, i., 4–9.

grievances were the tribute, the *alcabala*, and the rigor with which these taxes were collected. This rebellion reached its severest phase in Quito, where it is reported four hundred persons lost their lives in the hostilities which attended it. By the interference of the bishop and the clergy the commotion was allayed, and in the name of the king the audiencia promised a general armistice. During this rebellion at Quito, peace was maintained in other parts of the viceroyalty.

For the New Kingdom of Granada, as well as for other parts of the Spanish dominions, the most important event of the last half of the eighteenth century was the publication of the new commercial code. Another event of no little significance for the welfare of the people concerned was the separation of the territory of Venezuela from the viceroyalty. The difficulties of communication had made good government in this province, from Bogotá, practically impossible, whence the reestablishment of the individuality of Venezuela under a captain-general, in 1777, was in the interest of a more effective administration.

The fiscal reforms that were undertaken in the last quarter of the century aroused great dissatisfaction. This was made manifest in the uprising of 1781, which began in the town of

Socorro. At first the church lent its influence
to aid in the restoration of order, but ultimately
religious ceremonies failed to allay the popular
excitement. Prisoners were set at liberty,
efforts to preserve order were defied, and the
towns declared themselves free from the taxes
that had been imposed upon them. The most
objectionable of the fiscal reforms attempted
was the monopoly of tobacco assumed by the
government. The second phase of the revolution was the appointment by the inhabitants of
Socorro of four chiefs who were called captains-
general, and who were equal in authority.
Together they constituted the Supreme Council
of War. This example was followed by many
other towns, but all acknowledged Socorro's
superior revolutionary authority. The object
of the revolution was to abolish the monopolies
and the oppressive taxation which rested on
the agriculture and the industries of the
country; yet there was manifest no disposition
to throw off allegiance to the king of Spain.
Finally, through the intervention of Archbishop
Góngora and others, destructive hostilities were
prevented and peace was restored. The amnesty which was granted by the viceroy was
confirmed by the king, who wrote to Archbishop Góngora that the pacification of these
vast regions was due to him, whose authority
and discretion in this matter marked him as the

most illustrious member of the church in America. The recognition of Góngora's services caused him to be given also the highest secular office of the viceroyalty, which he administered with vigor and wisdom. He urged that mineralogists should be sent from Spain to aid in the development of the mines of the country; he founded a chair of mathematics in Bogotá; he established a botanical survey of equatorial America under the directorship of Dr. Jose Celestino Mutis; and prepared to defend the maritime provinces from attacks by the English. He undertook, moreover, to subdue the Indians of the Isthmus, to colonize the Mosquito Coast, and to relax the severe regulations concerning trade with foreigners. When he retired from his high office to return to Spain, he left the country in peace and prosperity.

A few years after the close of Góngora's administration, in 1791, the first periodical of New Granada began to be published. It was a weekly paper, and was called *Periodico de Santa Fé de Bogotá*. A large part of it was occupied by articles on literature and natural history. In it were announced some of the scientific discoveries of Dr. Mutis, to whom had been committed the directorship of the botanical survey. It continued to be published throughout the administration of Don Jose de

Ezpeleta, who was the viceroy from 1789 to 1797.

This northern region of South America enjoys the distinction of having witnessed the earliest phases of the movement for Spanish-American emancipation.

CHAPTER VIII

RIO DE LA PLATA

UNDER the laws which regulated the trade between Spain and America, and practically determined the routes of commerce, the valley of La Plata was on the extreme frontier, and its isolation helped to give it a larger measure of independence in its political development than was enjoyed by other colonies. Signs of this independence are seen in the frequent resort to election in filling the highest office of the colony, and in the persistent violation of Spain's restrictive commercial regulations.

The explorers of the valley of La Plata, like many of the other explorers of the eastern coast of America, hoped to find a passage through the newly discovered continent to the lands of the far East. Juan Diaz de Solis had this end in view when he entered the Rio de la Plata, as had also Cabot fifteen years later, in 1526.

But as Cabot proceeded into the narrow waters of the Paraná, the hope of reaching the Pacific by this route vanished. At the mouth of the Tercero, Cabot landed and laid the foundation of San Espiritu, the first Spanish settlement in this part of America. He left a number of men here, and proceeded on his voyage of exploration towards the north. He went first up the Paraná about one hundred and fifty miles beyond its junction with the Paraguay; then having returned to the confluence of these two great rivers, he ascended the Paraguay above the site on which was later founded the city of Asuncion. The hope of making this stream the highway over which should be carried the silver from Peru, induced Cabot to send messengers to Spain for further assistance. But this region, however fertile its soil and salubrious its climate, had few attractions for the Spaniards, and news from it aroused in them no enthusiasm. They were not anxious to possess lands which offered wealth only as the reward of the patient and persistent labor of the herdsman and the agriculturist ; consequently the reinforcements which Cabot asked for were never received. In 1530 Cabot returned to Spain to impress upon the king the importance of the territory he had added to the possessions of the crown. His services were recognized; he was raised again to the position of chief pilot; and in this office he continued, for the remaining thirty years of his life, the general director of Spanish expeditions to foreign lands.

The colony which Cabot had established at San Espiritu had the hard fate that attended all the early attempts to occupy the region of Rio de la Plata. The one hundred and seventy persons whom Cabot, on his return to Spain, left in possession of the settlement under Captain Nuño de Lara, rapidly disappeared before the hostility of the Indians, the lack of food, and the unfavorable conditions of the climate.

Although Cabot's account of his discoveries did not persuade the king to furnish means for extending them, it was nevertheless influential in moving Don Pedro de Mendoza to undertake the colonization of this new country. Mendoza was a nobleman of the emperor's household, who had won wealth and distinction as a soldier in the Italian wars. The supposed proximity of the valley of La Plata to the riches of Peru helped to convince the Council of the Indies that it was desirable to plant new colonies in this region as well as to maintain the one already established. But the necessary funds were wanting, and Mendoza offered to meet the expenses of an expedition, provided the king would confer upon him the title of *adelantado*, and make him governor of

the region he was to occupy. The privileges
which he demanded were granted to him and
to the successor whom he might designate.
On his part, Mendoza promised to take with
him one thousand men, a certain number of
ecclesiastics, who should labor for the conversion of the Indians; and also one hundred
horses and one hundred mares.[1] The contract between Charles V. and Mendoza provided, moreover, " that the ransom of any
foreign sovereign who might be captured,
though by law all belonging to the emperor,
should be divided among the conquerors, re-
serving to the crown only the royal fifth."[2]

The grant to Mendoza was not greatly unlike
the charters of commercial corporations in later
times. The holder sought to induce others to
take stock in the enterprise, and pointed to
the as yet unaccumulated funds as the source
of salaries and dividends. At the outset he
assigned to himself an annual salary of two
thousand ducats, and to others compensation
in keeping with the positions occupied. Don
Juan de Osorio was general-in-chief; Diego de
Mendoza, brother of the *adelantado*, was admiral of the fleet; Juan de Ayolas was chief
constable ; and George Mendoza and Ulric
Schmiedel were commanders of infantry. The

[1] Arcos, *La Plata*, 89 ; Pelliza, *Historia Argentina*, i., 58.
[2] Washburn, *History of Paraguay*, i., 15.

prestige of this expedition and the expectations which it awakened, induced more persons to apply for enlistment than Mendoza was able to accept. When the fleet finally set sail from the port of San Lucar, on the 1st of September, 1534, it carried not merely the stipulated one thousand, but two thousand five hundred persons, of whom one hundred and fifty were Germans, and the rest Spaniards.

The jealousy which arose among the members of this expedition during the voyage had a lamentable outcome in the assassination of Osorio. After this event the fleet went on to its destination, but through the death of Osorio the colony had lost its most conspicuous guaranty of success. In February, 1535, a landing was effected at the somewhat unpropitious site of the present capital of the Argentine Republic. A city was founded under the name of Santa Maria de Buenos Aires. A governor and judges had been appointed by the leader, and a municipal organization created, but the expected prosperity was not achieved. The stock of provisions was scanty, and the supply provided by the Indians was inadequate and uncertain. The hostility which was stirred up between the Indians and the Spaniards, through the stupidity of the colonial leaders, cut off this supply entirely. Inadequate food and unaccustomed exposure prepared the way for famine and pestilence, which rapidly diminished the ranks of the settlers. Of the two thousand five hundred colonists who came with Mendoza, there were only six or seven hundred survivors three years after their landing. At this time the colonists in the valley of the Rio de la Plata were distributed in three divisions: those who were at Buenos Aires; those at San Espiritu; and those who had gone northward with Ayolas in search of a way across the continent to Peru. San Espiritu, which had been devastated and abandoned, had been repeopled from Buenos Aires under the orders of Mendoza. In January, 1538, it was determined to gather together the remnants of the several settlements, and form a new colony. These earliest settlements were, therefore, deserted, and Asuncion, in Paraguay, was established. Isolated in the interior of the continent, and neglected by the mother country, the colonists at Asuncion undertook the management of their own affairs. Ayolas, who had been made the successor of Mendoza on the latter's return to Spain, had perished in the wilderness. In order, therefore, to provide a leader, or head, for the colony, recourse was had to an election by the members. Authority for this action was contained in the decree of Charles V., dated at Valladolid, September 12, 1537. With Ayolas's commission, there had been sent from

Spain letters-patent based on this decree, which provided for the election of a successor to Ayolas in case of his continued absence. Under this provision the settlers at Asuncion elected Irala governor. They organized a municipal administration, built a church, and placed it in charge of a Franciscan monk.

The rule of Irala is significant on account of the relations which he established between the Spaniards and the Indians, which were of such a nature as in a large measure to determine the character of the later population of Paraguay. In dealing with the Indians he decreed " certain laws which continued to exist long after him, in spite of the contrary regulation of the mother country." [1] Under these laws, " any Spaniard might undertake the conquest of a tribe, and become its master, holding it under the title of *encomienda.*" In case the individual's power was inadequate to the undertaking, the government might lend its aid; and the Indians thus brought into subjection were distributed among the soldiers as *mitayos* and *yanaconas.*

" The *mitayos* were under the obligation of personal labor during a specified time. The *yanaconas* were real slaves, but their master might not sell them nor abandon them in their old age; he was

[1] Arcos, *La Plata,* 105.

obliged to furnish them food, to clothe them, and to instruct them in the Christian religion." [1]

The immediate heir of the conqueror might inherit his *encomiendas*, but at the expiration of the second life, the Indians should be free. They might then work on their own account, but should be subject to a moderate poll-tax. Indians hitherto nomadic were compelled to adopt a settled life, to construct houses for themselves, and to submit to the municipal organization of a village or a town. A corregidor was appointed for the administration of justice, and the general affairs of the town were controlled by an *ayuntamiento* composed of two alcaldes and regidores. Although these settlements were composed exclusively of Indians, they were ordered in the form of Spanish municipalities. [2]

The period of Irala's administration is, moreover, noteworthy for the practice of polygamy, which at that time became general in the colony. A treaty was made with the Guarni Indians, in accordance with which they should grant to the governor seven wives, and to each of the soldiers two. Irala espoused the seven daughters of the principal chief.

[1] Arcos, *La Plata*, 105.
[2] Azara, *Descripcion é Historia del Paraguay y del Rio de la Plata*, i., 253.

" This matter appeared so natural to the Basque captain that, in his will, which has come down to us, he declared that he had taken the seven daughters of the *cacique* as wives, and requested that the children whom he had had by them should be considered as Spaniards." [1]

Through this extensive mingling of the blood of the two races, and the predominance of the Indian stock, the population of Paraguay became characterized by Indian rather than by Spanish traits.

In 1542, four years after the foundation of Asuncion by Irala, Cabeza de Vaca, as *adelantado*, and accompanied by about four hundred men, arrived, and entered upon his conquests in the region of Rio de la Plata. His instructions enjoined, among other things, that he should use great care to propagate the Christian religion; that he should take with him no advocates or solicitors; that the Spaniards and Indians should be permitted to trade freely with one another, without any interference on the part of the authorities; and that the captains should act as judges in all cases, but that there might be an appeal to the *adelantado*, and in the last resort to the Council of the Indies. On his arrival at Asuncion, Cabeza de Vaca was recognized by the colonists as the

[1] Arcos, 100.

head of all the Spanish establishments in this part of America, while Irala, as *maestro de campo*, held the second place. Under his administration, the neighboring Indians were subdued, and the material prosperity of the colony was increased; but Asuncion became divided into two factions. Those who had come to America with Mendoza, and who, under Irala, had founded Asuncion, stood in opposition to those who had arrived later under Cabeza de Vaca. The severity of the *adelantado's* administration tended to confirm his opponents in their opposition, and to weaken the allegiance of his followers. His attempts to abolish polygamy in the colony, and to prevent the ill-treatment of the Indians by those holding *encomiendas*, and other real or fancied grievances, led to his accusation and transportation to Spain for trial. He arrived in Seville in 1544, and, after years of waiting for a decision, a decree of exile to Africa was pronounced against him. Three years later, however, the decree was reversed, and the exile was recalled. Although his privileges were restored to him, he died before reaping any further advantage from them.

The prosperity of Paraguay during the first decade after the establishment of Asuncion suggested the desirability of giving it individuality in the ecclesiastical organization. In re-

sponse to a request from the Spanish court,
the pope created the bishopric of Paraguay,
and appointed Friar Juan de Barrios, of Toledo, bishop. By reason of old age and ill-
health, Bishop Barrios never assumed the duties
of his charge in America. In 1555, Pedro de
la Torre was appointed the second bishop of
the new diocese, and immediately proceeded
to take up his residence in Paraguay. His
jurisdiction extended over the whole valley of
La Plata; and the establishment of a centre of
ecclesiastical authority here helped to make
Paraguay independent of the viceroy of Peru
and the audiencia of Charcas. After the
division of this region into two provinces, in
1617, another bishopric was created, covering
the province of Buenos Aires, thus materially
limiting the territorial jurisdiction of the bishop
of Paraguay.

After the departure of Cabeza de Vaca, Irala
was elected governor of the colony for the
second time, and later was confirmed by the
crown in the exercise of his functions, under
the title of *adelantado*. He died in 1557,
having nominated Gonzalo Mendoza as his successor. On the death of Mendoza, the next
year, the colony had recourse once more to a
popular vote, and elected Vergara governor.
But not satisfied with the title conveyed by the
election, Vergara sought, at the hands of the

viceroy, the royal confirmation of the powers which he exercised by the will of the people. With this design, he went to Lima, but the fact of a popular election had little weight with the viceroy, who passed over the claims of Vergara and nominated one of his officers, Juan Ortiz de Zárate, *adelantado* of Paraguay. Wishing the direct approval of the crown, Zárate went to Spain, appointing Cacéres a deputy at Asuncion to act in his absence. This violation of the clearly expressed wish of the colonists revived the partisan conflicts which had filled the settlement with confusion in the time of Irala and Cabeza de Vaca. Bishop Torre led the friends of Vergara, and organized a conspiracy which resulted in embarking Cacéres for Spain. Confusion and anarchy followed, which were not allayed even by the arrival of Zárate with full powers derived directly from the crown. The new governor had engaged to introduce into the colony two hundred families, three hundred soldiers, four thousand cows, four thousand sheep, three hundred goats, and three hundred mares. In recognition of this obligation he had been made governor of the lands discovered by Cabot, with the right to appoint his successor. Before his death, in 1575, in accordance with this last provision, he designated as his successor the person who should marry a daughter whom he had left at

Chuquisaca. This proved to be Juan Torrés de Véra y Aragon. Not wishing to take up the reins of government till he should be able to fulfil the obligations under which Zárate had been appointed, Véra delegated his authority to Juan de Garay, under the title of lieutenant-governor and captain-general of Rio de la Plata. In 1576, Garay entered upon the performance of his duties, and continued to control the affairs of the settlements until he was killed by the Indians in 1584. Under him many colonies were established in different parts of the territory which later belonged to the Argentine Republic. Those which were founded in the northwestern part of this region derived their authority from the viceroy of Peru. Of these early foundations in the north, Tucuman and Santiago remain, while many of them have disappeared. But the most important of the settlements made by migration from the west was Cordova, founded in 1573, by Gerónimo Luis Cabrera. Cabrera's grant was received from the viceroy, Francisco de Toledo, and extended eastward to the river Paraná, and included both banks. The same day on which Cabrera founded Cordova, with the authority of the viceroy, Juan de Garay, under the authority of the governor of Asuncion, established the city of Santa Fé, on territory included in Cabrera's grant. This conflict of

claims was, however, set aside by Zárate's
confirmation of Garay's pretensions, and the
withdrawal of Cabrera to Cordova. Four
years after the death of Garay, Véra came with
his flocks and herds. But more important
than any of these events was the refounding
of Buenos Aires, in 1580.

In 1537, the first settlers at Buenos Aires
had abandoned five mares and seven horses.
These had multiplied extensively by 1580, and
their descendants were first brought into service by the soldiers of Garay, under whom the
city of Buenos Aires had been refounded.
The first sheep and goats introduced into Rio
de la Plata were brought from Charcas, in
1550. This kind of stock had, however, been
taken from Paraguay to Peru, and at this time
brought back across the continent. But the
most important basis of pastoral prosperity in
this region was the stock introduced by Véra,
and distributed among several of the settlements in the valley of La Plata.

During the period between the death of
Garay and the arrival of Véra, there was manifest among the settlements a strong particular-
istic spirit. In want of a recognized central
authority, the disrupting forces of anarchism,
strengthened by the isolation of the several
colonies, were conspicuously revealed. Véra,
however, succeeded in restoring order; but

four years after his arrival, he abandoned the government and went to Spain. After Torrés de Véra, it became customary for the governor to share his authority with a deputy.

" The jurisdiction of the deputies of the governor did not extend beyond the districts of the city for which they were severally appointed, including the settled surrounding country ; and each city within the territory of the governor had one of these deputies. The governors as well as their deputies exercised the functions of *justicia mayor*, and the latter were the immediate military chiefs of their districts." [1]

These officers served for periods of different lengths, being appointed for no predetermined terms. Certain matters of local administration were in the hands of the cabildos, or municipal councils. These bodies performed the ordinary functions of municipal corporations, their alcaldes administering justice in the first instance. The revenues were, however, managed by the royal officials, who also acted as judges in cases relating to these matters. The duties of police in the country were performed by *alcaldes de hermandad*, while these duties in the cities were performed by other appropriate subordinates.

[1] Zinny, *Historia de los Gobernadores de las Provincias Argentinas*, xv.

After the final retirement of Véra (1587
to 1591), recourse was had once more to an
election, which resulted in the choice of Hernando Arias de Saavedra, a native of Asuncion,
for governor. This time the wish of the inhabitants was regarded, and Saavedra's election
was confirmed by the crown. He held the
headship of the province from 1591 to 1594,
when the viceroy of Peru appointed Fernando
de Zárate to be his successor. In the brief
period of Zárate's rule, England sent three
ships with the purpose of taking possession of
the city of Buenos Aires. This early undertaking of the English is noteworthy, in view of
their later attempts to bring this rich region
under their authority. Zárate died in 1595,
and was succeeded by Juan Ramirez de Velasco
(1595 to 1597). Velasco had been viceroy of
Mexico and Peru, president of the Council of
the Indies, governor of Tucuman, and admiral
of the South Sea. After a brief rule of two
years, he returned, in 1597, to Tucuman, and
died there in 1606. Saavedra came to power
a second time in 1597, and yielded the govern-
orship in 1599 to Rodriguez de Valdes, who
had been appointed by the king.

Under Governor Valdes, the ecclesiastical
and political authorities were in conflict. The
commands of the governor, limiting the action
of the bishop, Thomas Vasquez de Liaño,

were overruled by the king, who approved and
confirmed the decision of the audiencia of
Charcas. Under this governor also, in 1601,
appeared the first physician and the first school-
master at Buenos Aires. Don Manuel Alvarez
presented to the municipal council his creden-
tials, asking that his salary for rendering medi-
cal aid to the inhabitants might be fixed, the
patients themselves being required to pay for
the medicines and all other necessary materials.
At this time also Francisco Victoria asked the
municipal council to asign him a house where
he might establish a school. Hitherto, for a
period of twenty years after its foundation, the
town of Buenos Aires had been without the
means of public instruction. The plan now
proposed by Victoria involved a monthly tuition of from one to two dollars for each child
instructed.

In 1602 Saavedra again became governor and
captain-general, appointed by the viceroy of
Peru, and remained in authority till 1609. During this period he undertook to restore order in
Asuncion, and made expeditions for discovery
to the Straits of Magellan and to the region of
the Chaco. He made provisions for the pres-
ervation and security of the archives of the
province. Notwithstanding the earlier attempt
to found a school at Buenos Aires, there were,
in 1608, no adequate means for instructing the

children of the city; and, on the invitation of
the municipal council, Felipe Arias de Mansilla
undertook to meet this want, charging those
who would learn to read a tuition fee of four
dollars and a half a year, and those who would
learn to write nine dollars. This venture appears not to have been successful, for, somewhat later, in 1610, a license to open a school
in the city was granted to Alexander Taurin,
and on this occasion a subsidy of twelve dollars
a year for each pupil was offered by the cabildo. The payment might be made quarterly
in flour, hides, tallow, or cattle.[1]

At this time not only the ordinances regulating the movement of goods were violated
at Buenos Aires, but also the ordinances established to control emigration. In view of this
violation of the law, a royal decree was issued
in 1610, imposing the penalty of death on
those persons who should help to secrete, or in
any way favor, passengers introduced without
a license from the king. And in the following
year it was prohibited to give lodging to any
who might come to the city without being able
to present a license from the governor.[2]

Saavedra was in authority for the fourth time
between 1615 and 1618. This period of his
administration was marked by two important
events. The first was the division of Rio de

[1] Zinny, i., xxiv. [2] *Ibid.*, xxxiii.

la Plata into two provinces[1]; the second event was the call extended to the Italian Jesuits, Maseta and Cataldini, who laid the foundations of the missions of Paraguay.

After the division, the new province of Buenos Aires embraced the cities of Buenos Aires, Santa Fé, Corrientes, and Concepcion del Bermejo; the other province comprised Guaira, or Ciudad Real, Villa Rica, and Santiago de Jerez. The name of Guaira was given to this province, but it continued to be generally known as Paraguay. As a separate province its first governor was Manuel de Frias, while the first governor of Buenos Aires was Diego de Góngora. After the close of Saavedra's rule, it became customary for the governor to be promoted to Buenos Aires from the province of Cordova; and after serving here to be transferred to some post on the Pacific. The position of viceroy of Peru or Mexico was the goal of political ambition in America. The governors at Buenos Aires during this period

[1] The proposed division was announced in a decree by the king in 1614, in the following form : " He tenido y tengo por bien que por tiempo y espacio de tres años mas ó menos ó lo que fuere my voluntad seais mi gobernador y capitan general en las dichas provincias del rio de la Plata . . . y habeis de tener y mando que tengais un teniente general en la provincia de Guairá y ciudad de la Asuncion, que es lo mas desviado del punto de Buenos Aires."—Pelliza, *Historia Argentina*, i., 82.

were usually military officers, who were appointed for five years, but whose term of service might be extended. Besides the gradual
development of the country subject to Buenos Aires, the attention of the governors
was directed to the encroachments of the
Portuguese.

The rule of Góngora as the first governor,
or captain-general, of Buenos Aires, after its
separation from the northern province of Paraguay, enjoyed the advantage of an extended
territory which had been won from the wild
tribes of the plains. Yet without mines and
with very little direct trade with Spain, life in
this province had few attractions. Everything
which ministered to taste or comfortable living
had to be imported, but on account of the
commercial restrictions then existing these
articles were entirely beyond the reach of the
bulk of the population. In contrast with the
conditions of civilized life which the denser
population of Peru made possible, the life of
the sparse and slowly increasing population on
the plains of Buenos Aires drifted towards a
state of barbarism. As long as legal restrictions
on commerce placed the people of Buenos Aires
in a disadvantageous position as compared with
the people of Peru, it was natural for them to be
impatient of their subordination to the authorities of Lima. On the other hand, the people

of Peru had grievances which provoked hostility towards the inhabitants of the region of La Plata. What was advantageous for one section was conceived to be disadvantageous for the other. The increasing contraband trade and the enlargement of the commercial privileges of Buenos Aires appeared to be an invasion of Peru's commercial monopoly and a menace to her material prosperity.

After the re-establishment of Buenos Aires, in 1580, its position was more favorable for industrial and commercial growth than that of Asuncion, yet in the beginning less favorable than that of Lima, in Peru. Even before the division of Rio de la Plata into two provinces, Buenos Aires had outrun the northern city, and become the commercial and political capital of the whole territory. Although easily accessible from Spain, yet the law which controlled the trade with the Indies made it the extreme frontier of the settlements which looked to Peru as a centre. Whatever European wares the inhabitants of Buenos Aires consumed, at a certain period, came to them from Peru. They were taken to Lima, either by way of the Isthmus, or by the southern sea route, and thence by caravans across the continent. This roundabout trade added greatly to the prices of goods from Europe, and practically compelled the people at a distance from

Lima to order their living in a manner so simple that little besides their own rude products would be demanded. It, however, gave to the settlements in the interior of the continent an importance which they would not otherwise have acquired. The conductors of the caravans carried on a private trade with the inhabitants of these settlements; by means of the caravans the settlers had facilities for communicating with both Buenos Aires and Lima, and with the various points along the way; and the halting-places of the caravans became markets for articles of food both for man and beast, which were produced along the route.

The expense of transporting goods by land from Lima to Buenos Aires stimulated the Portuguese to carry on a contraband trade. By bringing their wares directly from Europe, and smuggling them over the border to the Spanish river settlements, they could sell them at a small part of the necessary price of goods brought from Peru.

" During the first third of the eighteenth century, this clandestine traffic had acquired such proportions as to change in a marked manner the aspect of trade. Through it the progress of Buenos Aires became conspicuous to such an extent that the city of Lima not only had ceased to be the market

14

which supplied Rio de la Plata, Tucuman, and
Paraguay, but also that merchants came from Peru
to purchase at low prices the wares which the
Portuguese imported without paying duty."

To further this trade, the Portuguese, who had
established themselves at Bahia, Rio Janeiro,
and other points along the Atlantic coast, were
pushing their settlements towards the west and
south. By the establishment of the fort at
Colonia, the Portuguese not only placed themselves in a position to increase this contraband
trade, but also attempted to take possession of
important territory already claimed by the
Spanish. The indifference and inactivity of
Spain in these matters made it necessary for
the inhabitants of Buenos Aires to take the defence of their territory into their own hands.
An army of four hundred and sixty men was
organized, two hundred and sixty Spaniards
and two hundred Indians. One hundred and
twenty of the Spaniards were drawn from
Buenos Aires, sixty from Santa Fé, and eighty
from Corrientes. Under the leadership of Don
Antonio Véra y Mujica, they took possession
of the fort of Colonia and made the whole garrison prisoners, together with the women and
children at the post.

In the meantime another side of this game
was played in Europe. Finally brought to

consider the Portuguese encroachments, the
Spanish court demanded, through the minister
at Lisbon, reparation for the invasion of Spanish territory in America. The negotiations
dragged on till the arrival of news of the victory
of Antonio Véra, when they assumed a new
phase. Instead of regarding the fall of Colonia
as a justification of the Spanish cause, the
Portuguese pretended to find in this event a
violation of their own rights, and demanded
satisfaction. They even threatened Spain with
hostility, in case their demands were refused.
The Spaniards, however, were not willing to
have these differences lead to an open breach;
and therefore an agreement was made between
the two governments, which stipulated that
Colonia should be rendered to the Portuguese,
but on the condition that they should erect no
defensive works or make no permanent settlements on disputed territory, until special commissioners had determined whether Colonia
had been founded within or without the line
established by the treaty of Tordesillas. Questions on which the commissioners could not
agree should be referred to the pope for final
decision.[1]

When the commissioners met to adjust the
conflicting claims, Portugal wished delay, and
found some ground of objection to every prop-

[1] Calvo, *Coleccion de Tratados*, i., 176–189.

osition made by the opposite party. It was
finally determined to refer the matter to the
pope; but there were still objections, and
twenty years passed without a solution. After
the accession of the Bourbons to the Spanish
throne, Colonia was ceded to the Portuguese,
but the cession was revoked in 1704, and the
defence of Spanish rights was intrusted to the
viceroy of Peru. By his order the Portuguese
were driven out, and Colonia, with the artillery
and munitions of war which had been gathered
here, fell into the hands of the Spaniards. But
this was not the end of the contest. The
colony in dispute remained several years under
Spanish rule, but by the treaty of Utrecht was
once more ceded to the Portuguese. Under
this cession, the Portuguese claimed the country
between the Uruguay and Paraná rivers, but
the governor of Buenos Aires relinquished only
what might be demanded under a strict inter-
pretation of the treaty, namely, the little village
and a narrow belt of the surrounding territory.[1]
Remaining in the hands of the Portuguese,

---

[1] This treaty is printed in Calvo's *Coleccion*, ii., 163-177.
" In the king's letter dated at Madrid, January 27, 1720, and
directed to Bruno Mauricio de Zabala, governor and captain-
general of the city of Trinidad and Buenos Aires, he declares
that the territory of Colonia del Sacramento is limited to the
distance of a canon shot of a twenty-four pounder from the
plaza, and that neither the Portuguese nor any other nation
has the right to take possession of the ports of Maldonado and

Colonia became the place of deposit for foreign wares, and the centre of an extensive contraband trade in which Buenos Aires and other Spanish settlements had an advantageous part.

Throughout the controversy as to the title to Colonia and the neighboring regions, both parties recognized the necessity of abiding by the treaty of Tordesillas, but they were not agreed as to the starting point from which to begin to measure the three hundred and seventy leagues, a point which had been left without definite determination in the treaty. The Portuguese insisted on starting from the island of San Antonio, the most western of the Cape Verde group, while the Spanish were willing to make the island of San Nicolas, midway between the extremes, the point of departure. Another difficulty arose from the imperfection of the maps, and from a lack of the requisite knowledge and means for accurate measurement. After a number of unsuccessful attempts to fix the line of demarcation between the Spanish and Portuguese possessions in America, another treaty between the two

Montevideo nor to fortify themselves in them. The governor was, moreover, instructed to see that in determining this distance the piece used should be an ordinary twenty-four pounder, that it should be given a charge suitable to its calibre, that the powder should be such as is ordinarily used for cannon, and that the cannon should be discharged without elevating the muzzle."—Calvo, ii., 167, 242.

powers was finally formed in 1750, which, it
was agreed, should serve as the fundamental
rule for determining the limits of these possessions.   This treaty superseded whatever action
had hitherto been taken, whether by the bull
of Alexander VI., the treaties of Tordesillas,
Lisbon, and Utrecht, or by any other conven-
tions or promises, and determined that the
boundary between the two territories in question should be only that which was prescribed
by the articles of this treaty.   It confirmed to
Spain the Phillipine Islands and others adjacent
to them; and to Portugal the lands which the
Portuguese occupied on the Marañon and
Amazon rivers, as' well as those which they
held in the district of Matogroso.   It embraced, in Articles IV. to IX. inclusive, a de-
scription of the line of division, which appears
to have been drawn without reference to the
papal bull or the treaty of Tordesillas.   In
determining the right of possession, emphasis
was laid on the fact of priority of settlement.
The islands in the rivers along which the
boundary line passed belonged to the territory
whose shore was the nearer to the island in the
time of low water.   Colonia and its adjacent
territory were ceded to Spain, and this power
in return ceded to Portugal certain lands
which had hitherto been held by the Spanish.
Among these was the district between the

Ibicui and Uruguay rivers, occupied by seven towns, or reductions, which had been founded by the Jesuits. The missionaries of the territory thus set off to Portugal were permitted to remove, and to take with them their furniture and effects; they might also lead away the Indians, with a view of establishing them elsewhere. While the rivers were open to the free navigation of both parties, all trade across the frontier was strictly prohibited. When the summit ridge of a mountain chain was the boundary line, it was specially provided that no fortifications should be erected along this line; but that inviolability of this and all parts of the frontier were mutually guaranteed by the parties to the treaty.[1]

The principal difficulty in the way of carrying out the provisions of this treaty arose from the unwillingness of the people of the missions either to abandon their territory or to pass under the rule of the Portuguese. In the towns along the Uruguay there were about forty thousand Indians capable of bearing arms. Their organization under the Jesuits had some of the qualities of military rule; they had at least learned obedience to their leaders; but when they were informed that seven of their towns were to be turned over to the Portuguese, they gave unmistakable mani-

[1] Calvo, ii., 242–260.

festations of a spirit of rebellion. The Jesuits
petitioned both the Spanish and the Portuguese kings to delay the actual transfer till the
Indians had had opportunity to complete the
approaching harvest. The period was, in fact,
extended beyond the limit originally designated, for the Spanish commissioners did not
arrive in America until two years after the
treaty was signed. And in the meantime the
Jesuits persuaded the audiencias of Charcas
and Lima to advocate their cause with the
king. Yet in spite of all this, there appeared
to be a disposition on the part of the missionaries to obey the law. In an assembly of the
senior missionaries, however, " they declared,
with one single exception, that they did not
think it would be possible to do what was required of them." [1]   Yet in some cases attempts
were made by the people and their leaders to
move. But the difficulties which they encountered in these attempts led them to abandon
their project: and there was then nothing left
for them to do but to stand their ground.
When the commissioners appeared to mark the
line proposed by the treaty, they discovered a
determination on the part of the Indians not
to surrender their lands to the Portuguese. In
the hostilities which ensued, the Spanish and
Portuguese forces undertook to dislodge the

[1] Southey, *History of Brazil*, iii., 451.

Indians and Jesuits, and put the Portuguese in possession of the missions. After several years of bloody warfare the kings of Spain and Portugal agreed to abandon their undertaking; and on the 12th of February, 1761, the treaty of 1750 was annulled. This threw the relations between Spain and Portugal back to the status of 1749.

In this contest the Jesuits and their followers were victorious, but their victory made an unfavorable impression at the court of Madrid, where the throne was occupied by Charles III., the most liberal and vigorous of the Bourbon kings of Spain. On assuming the reins of power in 1759, two years before the Treaty of Limits was annulled, Charles III. was not without experience. For twenty years he had been king of the two Sicilies, and in this capacity had shown himself a wise and skilful administrator. This resistance of the Jesuits appeared to him as new evidence that their rich and powerful organization stood in the way of progress in America, and was not entirely without influence in provoking their expulsion in 1767.

By a decree dated August 8, 1776, Buenos Aires was raised to the dignity of a viceroyalty, and Pedro Antonio de Ceballos was made the first viceroy. He was at the same time given the title of lieutenant-general, and placed in command of a corps of nine thousand soldiers.

The fleet which conveyed him [1] and his army to America, consisted of one hundred and sixteen vessels. It left Cadiz in the autumn of 1776. The viceroy landed at Montevideo, and then proceeded to Colonia, which he captured, together with all the men and military equipment it contained. With this, Colonia ceased to be a Portuguese establishment, and was reincorporated into the territory of Montevideo. The sixty-three officers taken were sent to Rio Janeiro, while the common soldiers, most of whom had been carried thither from the Azores, were sent to Mendoza at the foot of the Andes. Here they became influential in developing the cultivation of the vine.

One of the effects of the establishment of the office of viceroy in Buenos Aires was an enlargement of the territory dominated from this capital. The province of Cuyo was separated

[1] The whole list of viceroys, with their terms of office, is as follows :

Pedro Antonio de Ceballos .	1776–1778
Juan Jose de Vertiz .	1778–1784
Nicolas del Campo .	1784–1789
Nicolas de Arredondo	1789–1795
Pedro Melo de Portugal · .	1795–1797
The Royal Audiencia and Antonio Olaguer Feliu	1797–1799
Gabriel de Aviles .	1799–1801
Joaquin de Pino .	1801–1804
Rafael de Sobremonte .	1804–1806
Santiago Liniers .	1806–1809
Baltasar Hidalgo de Cisneros .	1809–1810

from the captaincy-general of Chile, and incorporated in the new viceroyalty. The four provinces of Upper Peru, which were subject to the judicial authority of the audiencia of Charcas, were separated from the government of Lima, and embodied in the viceroyalty of Buenos Aires, which, by these additions, and by including the governments of Paraguay, Cordova, and Tucuman, came to comprise all the territory east of the Andes and south of the boundary of Brazil.[1]

During his reign as viceroy, Ceballos organized a superior provincial council at Buenos Aires, to which, under the second viceroy, Vertiz, were subordinated the municipal councils established in the four provinces of Rio de la Plata, Tucuman, Paraguay, and Cuyo. In the province of Rio de la Plata, there were created the municipalities of Buenos Aires, Corrientes, Santa Fé, Montevideo; in the province of Tucuman, Cordova, Santiago del Estero, San Miguel, Catamarca, Rioja, Jujui, and Salta; in the province of Paraguay, Asuncion; and in Cuyo, the municipalities of Mendoza, San Juan, and San Luis.[2]

The inhabitants of Buenos Aires found it in-

[1] Pelliza, i., 231.

[2] The following list embraces the names of the most important cities of the viceroyalty of Buenos Aires, together with the dates of their foundation :

convenient to resort to the audiencia which had been established in the city of La Plata. This difficulty was, however, set aside by the creation of a new audiencia in Buenos Aires, in 1782. The territory of its jurisdiction embraced the provinces of Buenos Aires, Tucuman, and Cuyo. The formal opening of this court was celebrated in August, 1785.

In July, 1809, Baltasar Hidalgo de Cisneros became the last of the Spanish viceroys in Buenos Aires. He governed until May, 1810, when the superior governmental council of the provinces of Rio de la Plata was organized. With this and the expulsion of Cisneros in June, the dominion of Spain over this region came to an end.

The population of the viceroyalty of Buenos

Buenos Aires I. in 1535, II., 1542		1580
Asuncion		1538
Santiago del Estero	(1549)	1553
Catamarca		1358
Mendoza		1560
San Juan de la Frontera		1560
San Salvador de Jujui		1560
San Miguel del Tucuman		1565
Cordova		1573
Santo Fé de la Vera Cruz		1573
Salta		1582
Corrientes		1588
Todos Santos de la Nueva Rioja		1591
San Luis de Loyola		1596
Concepcion del Uruguay		1783

Aires at the end of the colonial period is esti-
mated to have been about 800,000, of whom
nearly one half were Indians. This population,
so far as it was of European descent, was the
product of two streams of immigration, the
one coming directly across the Atlantic from
Spain, the other coming over the Andes from
Peru.[1] In many respects the settlers here
found their circumstances in sharp contrast
with those of Mexico and Peru. The natives
whom they had come to supplant were nomadic
tribes, with few traits indicating social development. There were no rich mines or stores of
gold and silver, and whatever wealth the
country had to offer could be had only as the
reward of persistent toil.

[1] Mitre, *Historia de Belgrano*, i., 5, notes certain chronological coincidences in the progress of these two streams. Diaz
de Solis discovered the Rio de la Plata from the Atlantic in
1515, and it was in 1513 that Balboa passed the Isthmus to the
Pacific. In 1527, Pizarro established himself provisionally on
the island of Gallo, and Cabot erected the fort of *San Espiritu*
on the shore of the Paraná. In 1535 the cities of Lima and
Buenos Aires were founded. Thirty-eight years later, in 1573,
the conquerors of Peru founded the city of Cordova, of Tucuman, while those of Rio de la Plata were founding the city of
Santa Fé, on the Paraná. A few years later the advance
guards of the two settlements met, thus establishing the over-
land communication between the Atlantic and the Pacific.

CHAPTER IX

THE JESUITS AND THE INDIANS

TWO noteworthy episodes in the colonial
history of Rio de la Plata were the socialistic experiment of the Jesuits and the English
undertaking against Buenos Aires. The former
illustrates the extreme view of the purpose of
missionary work in the Spanish colonies; the
latter, the persistent design of the English to
establish their authority in South America.

To the Jesuits who proposed to convert the
Indians to Christianity, and to bring them to
an orderly social life,

" it did not seem desirable that their young neo-
phytes should be brought into close contact with
the residents already settled; it suited their ideas
better that they should be so separated as to form
an isolated community, living on their own resources, and only mingling with the population with

the aim of Christianizing it. For this design the
vast wildernesses beyond the Paraná seemed in
every way to be adapted to their requirements.
The locality was so far removed from the ordinary
haunts of men that in order to reach their settlements it was necessary to cross the marshes of Nem-
bucu or the Ibera lagoon, if not to venture over the
Apipe rapids, and only a few would be tempted to
undertake the journey. Thus the missionary settlement was at once well sheltered, and quite secure
from intrusion from outsiders." [1]

It was proposed that here the Indians should
be associated with the fewest possible persons
besides members of their own race, and should
yet be advanced to civilization. To secure this
end the Jesuits had made their first settlements
in the upper valley of the Paraná, but the
hostility of the Indians led them to abandon
these earliest posts, and to re-establish themselves in the region now known as the province
of *Missiones.* Here a number of villages were
founded, which were called reductions. The
Indians in each village or pueblo were subject
to the authority of two resident Jesuits.

" The one called the cura had either been provincial or rector in their colleges, or was at least a
grave *padre.* He did not exercise the essential

---

[1] De Bourgade la Dardye, *Paraguay*, 15.

functions of a priest, and frequently did not know the language of the Indians. He occupied himself only with the temporal administration of all the property of the pueblo, of which he was the absolute director. The spiritual department was confided to another Jesuit, called *compañero*, or vice-cura, subordinate to the first. The Jesuits of all the pueblos were under the superintendence and vigilance of another, named the *Superior* of the missions, who had, moreover, the power to confirm from the pope. To control these pueblos they had no laws, either civil or criminal ; the only rule was the will of the Jesuits. Though in each pueblo there was an Indian called a corregidor, and others called alcaldes and regidores, that formed a municipal body, like what they have in the Spanish colonies, no one of them exercised the least jurisdiction, and they were only instruments that served to execute the will of the curas, even in criminal cases. The curas who inflicted the punishments were never cited before the king, nor before any of the ordinary tribunals. They compelled the Indians of both sexes, and of every age, to labor for the community, without permitting any person to labor at all for himself. All must obey the orders of the cura, who stored up the produce of the labor, and who had the charge of supplying food and clothing to all. From this it is seen that the Jesuits were absolutely masters of everything ; that they completely disposed of the surplus stock of the whole community ; and that all the Indians were equal, without any distinction, and unable to possess any private property." [1]

The cura and the vice-cura were appointed, under the royal authority, by the governor of the province, after they had been presented by the provincial of the Jesuits, and been recommended as having the qualifications necessary to the discharge of their duties; but they were assigned to their respective churches by the bishop. In the practical management of the affairs of the pueblos, there was no appeal from the decisions of the Jesuits to any other Spanish authority. [2] But in case it became necessary to impose capital punishment for some atrocious crime, " for which it would be difficult to produce precedents, the affair was carried to the tribunal of the governor of the province, in whom alone was vested the power of condemning an Indian to death." [3] According to Muratori, if one were guilty of a fault that might produce a scandal, the guilty person was

" brought in a penitential habit to the church, to beg pardon of God in a public manner for the of-

[1] Azara, quoted by Washburn, i., 100. Some of the conclusions reached by Azara concerning the Jesuits and the Indians may be found in English in MacKinnon, *Steam Warfare in the Parand*, ii., 245–281.

[2] Azara, i., 275.

[3] Muratori, *Missions of Paraguay*, 126.

fence, and a penance was enjoined on the offender.
He was then brought out to the square, where he
suffered in public a punishment suited to the nature
of the offence." [1]

Inasmuch as much of our information concerning the Jesuit missions is derived from the
Jesuits themselves, allowance must be made
for the roseate atmosphere through which their
affairs are sometimes seen. We are told that
after the punishment had been inflicted, the
criminal " kissed the hand that had punished
him," and thanked God that by this slight
correction he had been helped to avoid eternal
punishment; and that " men, and even women,
who had secretly committed the fault that they
saw punished in another, ran of their own ac-
cord to the regidor and accused themselves,
withal earnestly begging to suffer the same
penance." However credible these statements
may be, for some of the things reported the
critical historian has need of further corrobo-
rative evidence.

In addition to the revenues derived from the
pueblos for ecclesiastical purposes, the royal
treasury was expected to make substantial con-
tributions. These covered, among other things,
three hundred piastres each for the evangelical
workers sent from Europe to Paraguay by the

[1] Muratori, 70.

king's authority; the cost of their passage; and
ten thousand piastres annually for the support
of the missionaries in Paraguay. The king
provided, moreover, the necessary sacred ornaments and a bell for each church; also the wine
used at the altar, and the oil which was burned
day and night before the altar; and finally one
hundred and forty piastres to purchase drugs
for the use of each pueblo.

At first the public buildings of the pueblo
were very simple. The most important of
these was the church.

The missionaries' house adjoined the church;

"next are the storehouses, and public granaries,
where all sorts of grain, the herb *Cua*, cotton, and
other provisions, are stored up in common, to be
distributed to the people yearly as they want.
Contiguous hereto are built the shops and work-
houses for the different trades; then follow the
houses of the Indians, disposed like stalls in a
market-place. The streets are laid out by a line.
The houses have only a ground floor, and consist
in a square hall, where all the family is lodged.
They are made of reeds plastered with mortar, and
without any chimneys or windows; and so have no
aperture but the door, to admit light, and to let
out the smoke of a constant fire kept in the middle
of the room."

Usually when civilized and uncivilized peoples are brought into peaceful contact, the

ruder people acquires knowledge of many of the arts of civilized life by observing their new neighbors. A fault in the organization of the reductions as centres for the development of civilization was that it kept the Indians in isolation; their only instructors in the arts of enlightened society were the missionaries, who, by reason of their peculiar training and an abnormal position in the world, could not be expected to be the most efficient guides. Instead of having an enlightened society as a model, they were directed by the precepts of the missionaries, and by the neophyte superintendents who were set over them to " observe whether they work, sow, and reap, in due time; whether measures are taken to make the provisions of grain hold out from one harvest to the next; and to conclude whether the cattle be well looked after." [1]

Florentine de Bourges, who visited the missions of Paraguay in 1712, found, in the reductions which he observed, that the whole product of the year was carried to the public granary, and that a number of persons was appointed, whose business it was to take an exact account of all that was brought into the magazines.

" At the beginning of every month all these corn officers give out what is necessary to the chiefs of

[1] Muratori, 142.

the several quarters of the town, by whom each family is allowed what is sufficient for a month's subsistence. There is in like manner an equal distribution of other provisions. A set number of sheep and oxen is daily brought to town, which are slaughtered and delivered up to the proper officers, from whom the rest of the inhabitants are to receive their allowance." [1]

To the same effect is the statement of Don Felix de Azara. He made extensive investigations concerning the natural and geographical conditions of Paraguay, during a long residence there in the last half of the eighteenth century, and described the life at the missions, and pointed out its socialistic character. He affirmed that the parish priest gave no license to anyone to work for his own special advantage,

" all without distinction of age or sex being compelled to work for the common interest of the mission, while the priest took upon himself to provide food and clothing for all. And to this end all the products of agriculture and industry were gathered into public store-houses," [2]

while the unconsumed surplus was sent to the Spanish settlements and exchanged for tools

---

[1] *Lettres edifiantes*, xiii., letter by Florentine de Bourges, 1712 ; see also Muratori, *Missions of Paraguay*, 292.

[2] Azara, i., 276.

and such other articles as they needed. The inference drawn from the observed facts was that the priest controlled the common surplus, " and that no Indian could aspire to hold private property." Under this system the stimulus to the exercise of the individual powers was removed, since the same provision of food, clothing, and other means of enjoyment was made for the lazy, stupid, and vicious, as for the diligent, skilful, and virtuous.[1] The desire to have the community rich was not a powerful motive to individual action in the case of the habitually improvident Indian; yet this improvidence, or the assumption that the Indians would not properly feed their families or preserve the surplus of a time of plenty for a time of scarcity, was among the reasons offered for the existence of the socialistic organization of the missions.

When it was suggested after a century and a half that the Indians ought to be able to maintain themselves in an individualistic society, the fathers urged that this experiment should not be made on account of the incapacity of the Indians, and the evils which would result to their morals and religion if they were brought into contact with the Spaniards. It was proposed, however, to give them partial independence, to assign them certain pieces of land, and

[1] Azara, i., 279.

two days in the week for its cultivation, and by this means to accustom them gradually to self-control in freedom and the absolute possession of property. It is possible that the unwillingness of the priests to be deprived of power and position made them desire the status of the Indians to remain unchanged.[1]

After the expulsion of the Jesuits,[2] in 1767,

[1] In the statement of Azara, setting forth the position of the priest in the missions, is the following : " The priests and companion or vicar had houses which they did not enter in the ordinary way, but through the great enclosed garden from the school ; they never went out of them to walk in the streets of the town, nor to enter the house of an Indian ; they did not allow themselves to be seen by the women, nor by others except those to whom it was necessary to give their orders.. If an invalid needed spiritual aid, he was taken from his miserable house to a clean room near the school, set apart for this purpose, and the vicar, carried in a sedan, with great pomp, administered to him there the holy sacrament. When they appeared in the church, although it was only to say mass, it was with the greatest possible ostentation, clothed with the greatest richness, surrounded and assisted by clerks, acolytes, and musicians, whose number, I believe, did not fall below a hundred. All their churches were the largest and most magnificent in that part of the world, full of splendid altars, pictures, and gilding ; the ornaments could not be better or more precious in Madrid or Toledo."—*Descripcion e Historia de Paraguay y del Rio de la Plata*, i., 283.

[2] The expulsion of the Jesuits occurred during the period of Bucareli's administration. They were embarked in the man-of-war *La Venus*, commanded by Gabriel de Guerra, and two private vessels called *San Estevan* and *Pajaro*. The whole number sent from the region of Rio de la Plata, including the Indian missions, was three hundred and ninety-seven.

the Indian population of the missions declined rapidly. De Doblas has rendered concerning the Indians a more favorable judgment than that expressed by Humboldt. In his view the bulk of this population manifested fair ability in whatever it undertook; but the power of the Indians in imitation exceeded their capacity of original creation. They were humble and obedient, and submitted readily to the commands of those whom they recognized as superiors. This was said of them after some generations of life in the missions. Like all uncivilized peoples, they appeared lazy when judged by the standard of civilization. They were ambitious to learn, but in their isolation, with no object lessons of the higher forms of society, and without a knowledge of the language of their superiors, the most direct avenues to enlightenment were not open to them. Though submitting formally to the practices of the church, they yet regarded with indifference certain lines of conduct which civilized men consider as grossly immoral. If they were seldom overcome in drunkenness, it was not from lack of inclination but from lack of opportunity. They delighted in music or rhythmical noise, and were pleased to have it as an accompaniment of all their tasks. They were patient and uncomplaining under their severest work; and sickness and suffering they bore with calmness and almost stoical severity. In their houses, or huts, they were careless of the conventionalities of clothing, and in all matters of domestic life and labor they cast the heaviest burdens on the women. Yet even under the inhuman treatment which the women often received, they seldom complained ; perhaps they were aware that complaints would only bring additional grievances.

The community of goods which was maintained in the several mission towns made parents careless of the education of their children, as also of their food and clothing. The zeal which arises from the possibility of acquiring, holding, and bequeathing property was wanting. The surplus of the common stock which remained after the wants of the inhabitants had been met, was sent to markets outside of the province. The wares exported were for the most part sent to Buenos Aires.

The expulsion of the Jesuits marks a turning-point in the history of these mission towns. Hitherto both their spiritual and temporal affairs had been in the hands of priests. At this time they were brought under a new system of administration, which was determined by ordinances formed by Francisco Bucareli, governor and captain-general of Buenos Aires. Under this new system, there was a governor, subordinated to the government of

Buenos Aires. Provision was also made for
three deputies of the governor, whose powers
were similar to those of the governor in their
respective districts. Besides these general
officers, there was appointed a Spanish administrator for each town, who had in charge
its material and temporal interests; and two
ecclesiastics, a priest and an assistant, who
directed its spiritual interests. The priest received a stipend of three hundred dollars, the
assistant two hundred and fifty dollars, and the
support of both was furnished by the town.
By a royal decree of 1778, the stipend was
diminished and fixed at two hundred dollars
for each. These officers were intended as a
substitute for the Jesuit officers and priests.
The formal Indian municipal organization was
continued with whatever functions had previously belonged to it.

Under the new order the material well-being
of the missions declined; for the Indians ceased
to be efficient when the specific prompting of
the priest was withdrawn, and the Spaniards
who were placed in charge of the missions were
scarcely more efficient than the Indians. In
the course of time the government recognized
the damage that was being inflicted and undertook to repair the injury.

" For this purpose all the useless administrators
were removed, and their places filled by others of

superior ability and better conduct. They undertook to oblige the Indians to work, laying especial
stress on the re-establishment of the farms, and
finally adopted all those means which appeared
efficient." [1]

Although a military governor was placed
over all the missions of Paraguay and Uruguay,
the internal organization of the several missions
was not greatly changed. The prospects of
the Indians, however, were modified.

" The Jesuits were skilful, moderate, and economical ; they looked upon the towns as their own
work, and regarded them as their peculiar property
and sought to improve them. The secular governors and the administrators appointed by them,
besides not having the intelligence of the Jesuit
fathers, regarded the goods of the communities as
a mine which they might not be allowed to work
but a short time. It is not strange, therefore, that
the communities were impoverished,"

and that the Indians deserted, to the great advantage of certain neighboring settlements,
but greatly to the disadvantage of the ancient
missions. [2]

The fate of the missions was what might
have been expected, in view of their influence

[1] De Doblas, *Memoria historica, geographica, politica y
economica sobre la Provincia de Misiones*, 19
[2] Azara, i., 286.

on the individual Indian. With his subsistence assured;

" released from continual struggles against hostile powers, from conflicts with the elements and man, he led a more monotonous life, less active, and less fitted to inspire energy of mind, than the habits of the wild or independent Indian. He possessed that mildness of character which belongs to the love of repose ; not that which arises from sensibility and the emotions of the soul. The sphere of his ideas was not enlarged, where, having no intercourse with the whites, he remained a stranger to those objects with which European civilization has enriched the New World." [1]

He was especially fitted to become the victim of absolute authority. He was overwhelmed in a kind of mental and moral imbecility, and was thoroughly submissive under any power that assumed dominion over him. Characters like those produced in the missions made possible the later reigns of Francia and Lopez. [2]

---

[1] Humboldt, *Travels*, i., 300.

[2] The evil effects of the missions were repeatedly pointed out by Humboldt. Writing at the close of the colonial period, he said, " the effects of this insulated system have been such that the Indians have remained in a state little different from that in which they existed, while yet their scattered dwellings were not collected around the habitation of the missionary. Their number has considerably augmented, but the sphere of their ideas is not changed. They have pro-

By the ordinance which established the secular authority over the missions, it was provided that there should be held every year in Candelaria a general council composed of the governor, the deputies, the corregidors, and the administrators of all the towns; but the meeting aimed at in this ordinance was never held.

Under this new order of things, there was a secular administrator who had charge of the temporalities, and two ecclesiastics who taught the Indians, administered the holy sacraments, and afforded them spiritual guidance. By this arrangement, authority which had been centralized in a single hand was divided between the two classes of agents.

" The Indians, accustomed to obey only their priests, regarded the commands of the administrators with indifference in the beginning, to such an extent that nothing was done without first consulting the *padre.* From these beginnings arose serious controversies between the priests and the administrators, which contributed in great measure to the ruin of the towns, as Francisco Bruno de Zavala complained in the report which he made to the king in 1774. The priests took possession of the principal houses, the already mentioned colleges, not

gressively lost that vigor of character and that natural vivacity which in every state of society are the noble fruits of independence."— *Travels to the Equatorial Regions of America*, i., 201.

permitting the administrators to live in them ; they did the same with their gardens and their fruit, and presumed to dispose of everything arbitrarily." [1]

Attempts were made to inform the Indians that they owed obedience in spiritual matters to the priests and in temporal matters to the administrators; yet the conflict of authority and commands led them into uncertainty as to their proper superiors. Sometimes the priests punished them for obeying the administrators, and at other times the administrators punished them for obeying the priests; and between the two they found that their lines had not fallen in pleasant places.

A suggestive phase of the socialistic character of the mission towns was seen in the fact that at the age of four or five years the boys were placed in charge of the community. For their immediate care there were appointed from among the Indians two or more persons, called alcaldes or secretaries of the boys, whose duty it was to gather them all together early in the morning, and take them to the church for prayers. They then sent them to their several tasks. At two or three o'clock in the afternoon they returned with them to the church, and after prayers permitted them to go to their homes. The trades or professions of the boys were not

[1] De Doblas, 25.

determined by themselves or their parents, but by the public authorities. A committee of persons selected those who were thought to be best fitted to achieve success in the several occupations. With reference to the girls essentially the same course was pursued. At the age of ten or twelve, they were placed in charge of two or more old Indians. But this method of training removed them from the control of their parents without providing any efficient substitute, and the result was a very early moral deterioration. When the youth and the girls reached a certain degree of maturity, they were married, either under the direction of their parents, or of the priests, or under the stimulus of passion, but always without sentiment or intimate acquaintance, and with a stolid indifference, which continued to mark the relation between husband and wife, and between parents and children.

It was not to be expected that Indians brought into villages from the freedom of the forest would immediately become careful to preserve property. They were not only indifferent to accumulation, but in the service of the community they had a peculiar aversion to the tasks that were imposed upon them. For each of the several occupations it was, therefore, necessary to appoint overseers, and then even overseers of overseers. They rarely began

work before nine o'clock in the morning, and
concluded their labors about three in the afternoon, " having done little more than nothing."
In gathering the products, at least half of
them were stolen by the several grades of persons concerned in the harvest. This form of
corruption which belonged to the later state of
the missions was encouraged by the fact that
the corregidors and the other members of the
cabildo received no salary or compensation for
the services of their offices.   In addition to all
the other ills that were overwhelming the missions in the later decades of the eighteenth
century, came another indication of dissolution
in the desertion of large numbers of the Indians.[1]

[1] De Doblas, 29–33.

CHAPTER X

THE KING AND THE CHURCH, ILLUSTRATED BY THE ECCLESIASTICAL ESTABLISHMENT IN MEXICO

THE position of the king of Spain as the supreme patron[1] of the church in Spanish America was involved in his character as monarch. In the laws relating to this subject, this position is described, and the various features of the king's authority in ecclesiastical matter positively set forth, which may be illustrated by reference to Mexican history. In a royal decree of 1574, it was declared that " the right of patronage of the Indies is, alone and undivided, forever reserved to us and our royal crown, and may not be alienated from it either wholly or in part." In keeping with this power, the bull of Julius II. concerning the

---

[1] " No puede darse Real Patronato mas completo, mas singular y privativo, que el que gozan los Reyes Catolicos en su Estado de las Indias."—Parras, *Gobierno de los Regulares de la America*, i., 3.

patronage conceded primarily that in the regions discovered, or which in the future might be discovered, no churches, monasteries, or pious places might be established without the consent of the king. It conceded also the power to present suitable persons for the metropolitan churches and the other cathedrals already erected or which in the future might be erected, and for all other ecclesiastical livings whatsoever.

In the decree of 1574, Philip II. based the claim of the Spanish crown to the right of patronage in the Indies on the fact that the New World had been discovered and acquired by the crown, and that churches had been built and endowed in it at his expense and at the expense of his predecessors, the Catholic kings, and also as having been granted by the popes. The bull of Julius II. had been preceded by that of Alexander VI. " conceding to the Catholic kings all the tithes of the state of the Indies, under the condition of endowing the churches, and providing the priests with proper support." [1] The king, however, transferred his right to receive the tithes to the bishops, the churches, the hospitals, and other institutions destined to receive them. To this end the mass of the tithes was divided into four parts. Two of these parts were assigned

[1] Parras, i., 6.

in equal shares to the prelate and the chapter;
and the sum of the other two parts was sub-
divided into nine divisions and further distributed. In this distribution, two of these
secondary parts were reserved for the king[1];
three were divided between the hospital and
the fund for building churches; and from the
remaining four was drawn the support of the
curates, while the rest was given to the prebendaries. In case of a vacancy in the position
of a prelate, the tithes reverted to the king;
but he relinquished them in favor of the church,
one half going to maintain the worship during
the vacancy, the other half to the succeeding
prelate. It has been set down to the credit
of the king that having a legitimate claim to
all the tithes of the Indies, he distributed them
for the maintenance of the church, and for
other pious purposes. The quality of patron
has, moreover, been cited as the most brilliant
feature of the Spanish crown; and to the wise
exercise of the prerogatives of the kings in this
regard has been attributed the vast extension
of the dominions of Spain in America.[2]

In accordance with a papal bull issued by
Leo X., the first bishopric of Cuba was created,
in 1518, in Baracoa, which at the time the

---

[1] On the disposition of these parts, see *Recop. de Indias*,
Lib. i., Tit. xvi., Ley 24.

[2] Parras, i., 7-9 ; *Recop. de Indias*, Lib. i., Tit. xvi., Ley 23.

bishopric was suggested possessed the only
church on the island. But before the decree
had been made and carried out other towns had
been planted, and Santiago had become the
residence of the governor and the principal
men of the colony. In 1522, the town of Santiago was made the capital of the bishopric.
The position of bishop was first offered to Ber-
nardino Mesa, and then to Julian Garcés, but
it is not known that either of these ever actually
performed any of the functions of the office.
The first person consecrated bishop of Cuba
was John De Witt, who was born in the Nether-
lands. He, however, never went to Cuba, but
undertook some of the duties of his office while
at Valladolid. From this city, on the 8th of
March, 1523, he issued instructions for the
organization of the chapter of the cathedral of
Santiago. In 1525, he retired from the bishopric, and this see remained vacant till 1536. In
the meantime the ecclesiastical affairs of the
island fell into disorder.

In the beginning, the island of Jamaica fell
within the jurisdiction of the bishop of Cuba,
but it was soon separated from the Cuban
diocese, and erected into a mitred abbacy.
Subsequently an effort was made by Bishop
De Witt to have it reincorporated in his
bishopric, but in this he was unsuccessful.[1]

[1] Pezuela, *Historia de la Isla de Cuba*, i., 123-125.

Under decrees of the church authorizing the various religious orders to undertake work for the conversion of the natives in the Indies, a rapidly increasing number of ecclesiastics found their way to the New World. As early as July, 1524, we find Martin de Valencia in Mexico assembling the friars who had come with him from Spain and those already in the country for the purpose of assigning to them their several fields of labor. The region about the City of Mexico was divided into four districts, and to each four friars were assigned, while Valencia himself devoted his efforts to the capital. In these districts convents were established, the religious life organized, and plans matured for bringing the natives into submission to ecclesiastical authority.

The Franciscan and Dominican friars had extended their missionary efforts over a large part of New Spain before these regions were formally brought under the jurisdiction of the organized church. In 1519, Julian Garcés was made bishop of Cozumel, an island off the coast of Yucatan. There were found to be very few settlers within the limits of this bishopric, even after it had been extended to the neighboring peninsula, and in 1526 it was made to embrace the districts of Tabasco, Vera Cruz, and Tlascala. The official seat of the bishop was in Tlascala. About the time that

Garcés appeared in Tlascala to assume the duties of his charge, another bishopric was created with the City of Mexico as its capital; and, in December, 1527, it was bestowed upon Juan de Zumárraga. The new bishop was also charged with the power of protector of the Indians; but in attempting to perform the duties implied in this title, he found himself opposed not only by the Spanish settlers but also by the audiencia.

The fact that the spiritual teachings of the bishop and his followers were not heeded by men of his own nationality, that organized authority was employed to further measures of injustice, and that great wrongs were inflicted on the natives by the Spanish settlers, helped to weaken the moral influence of those who pretended to preach a gospel of peace and good-will to all men. The authorities in Spain, however, appeared to have confidence in Zumárraga, and sought his advice concerning the government of the Indians, and the means of improving their condition. For this purpose he was recalled to Spain in 1532. On this occasion his plans and previous labors were approved, his title of protector of the Indians was confirmed, and the audiencia was instructed to co-operate with him in carrying out his designs. On this occasion, also, he was solemnly consecrated as the first bishop of Mexico. This ceremony was performed at Valladolid on the 27th of April, 1533; and before he returned to Mexico he issued from Toledo a letter appointing the members of the chapter of the cathedral, and establishing rules for the government of his diocese. The chapter as organized consisted of a dean, archdeacon, precentor, chancellor, treasurer, ten canons, and six prebendaries, whose salaries ranged from thirty-five to one hundred and fifty dollars a month.

In 1534, the year of Zumárraga's return to America, New Spain was divided into four political divisions, which were designated as the provinces of Mexico, Michoacan, Goazacoalco, Miztecapan. In addition to the two bishoprics which had already been created, two others were now formed, and the four were known as Mexico, Michoacan, Tlascala, and Oajaca. These were made to correspond to four political provinces; but their boundaries were only imperfectly determined. It was ordered that each bishopric should embrace all points within a radius of fifteen leagues from its cathedral town taken as a centre; that the intervening territory should be divided equally between the adjoining sees; and that if any principal town lay near a boundary, its district should belong to the diocese in which the town lay. Of the new bishoprics, that of Oajaca was conferred upon Juan Lopez de Zárate, while that of Michoacan was given to Vasco de Quiroga, who had been a member of the audiencia, and who took priestly orders after his appointment.

In the course of time other bishoprics were created, and that of Mexico was made an archdiocese. The papal bull confirming this change was issued July 8, 1547. The jurisdiction of the archbishop of Mexico was extended over the bishops of Tlascala, Michoacan, Oajaca, Nueva Galicia, Yucatan, Guatemala, Chiapas, Honduras, and Nicaragua. The position of archbishop was offered to Zumárraga, but he declined it on account of his great age. A few days after the arrival of the documents conveying to him the appointment, he died in his eightieth year, on June 3, 1548. After the death of Zumárraga, the archbishopric was offered in succession to several distinguished prelates, but it was declined by them, and remained vacant until the appointment of Alonso de Montufar, in 1551.[1] The organization of the church in Mexico was fairly complete after the archbishop had been installed in office, and there was a disposition on the part of the officers of the church to maintain

[1] Montufar held the position of archbishop till 1569. After him there were twenty-six other archbishops during the period of Mexican dependence on Spain. See Alfaro, *Historia de la Ereccion del Obispado de Mexico*, 9-12. Mexico, 1866.

what were regarded as their prerogatives. The religious orders claimed independent jurisdiction, but when the church had so far extended itself as to be able, without difficulty, to exercise its functions on all parts of the kingdom, the conflicting claims of the regular and secular clergy became especially manifest. The right to receive tithes and tributes was a conspicuous point in contention. The regulars, moreover, complained that the archbishop and the bishops were reluctant to ordain members of the orders, and that consequently there were in these orders few priests who were efficient in their labors with the natives. They further complained that even their ordained priests were denied the right to administer the sacraments, being limited in their functions to instructing the Indians and celebrating mass. They brought their grievances to the attention of the pope and by a bull issued March 24, 1567, were granted the right to administer the sacraments in the Indian towns. But in spite of this authorization by the pope, the secular clergy refused to concede the point, and stood so vigorously in the opposition that the friars were commanded by the pope, in 1583, to renounce their rights in this regard; but this did not end the controversy, for both parties appealed to the crown.

Yet there appears to have been a studied at-

tempt to prevent conflicts of interests between
the regular and secular clergy. The bishops
and archbishops were instructed neither to establish parish priests in Indian towns and reductions where there existed monasteries and
monks holding curacies, nor to found a monastery of any order whatsoever, where parish
priests had already been established; and if
" monks should preach in the towns where
there were parish priests, the archbishop or the
bishop should request them to go elsewhere or
return to their monasteries," and to confine
their missionary labors to places where it might
be necessary or possible, in accordance with
the law, and under the proper authority, to
found a monastery or monasteries.[1]

No monk could become a curate or parish
priest, except through a special nomination by
the vice-patron, and in case of such nomina-
tions it was required that there should always
be due recognition of the authority of the king
as the supreme patron. The person thus promoted was required to know the language of
the natives he was expected to teach. His
fitness in this and other respects was determined
by an examination held by the prelate of the
diocese or by persons of his appointment. In
appointing the priest, the name was sent to the
viceroy, president, or governor, who exercised

[1] *Recop. de Indias*, Lib. i., Tit. xiii.

the functions of royal patron in the name of the king. The necessary support of priests of this class were stipends furnished by prelates of the regulars.[1]

In 1600, there were in New Spain four hundred convents of the several orders ; four hundred districts in charge of clergymen. Besides these, the convents and the important churches had other churches dependent on them, where religious services were held from time to time, and where the natives were taught the Christian doctrines.

Not only the archbishops and bishops, but also the viceroys and governors were instructed " by all possible means to seek continually to know the monks who were in their districts " ; and they should inquire if more were needed, keeping an account of the number admitted, and of the special religious work they were called to perform. The provincials of all the orders were required to reside in the Indies; and each was expected to keep a list of all the monasteries in his district, and of all the persons belonging to them. Any commissioner taking monks to America had to report to the Council of the Indies their names, ages, places of birth, and the provinces or monasteries in Europe from which they came. After they had been approved by the council, their names

[1] *Recop. de Indias*, Lib. i., Tit. xv., Leyes 1–14.

were also recorded in the Casa de Contratacion at Seville. The expenses of supporting and transporting them were met by the royal treasury through the Casa de Contratacion. Great care was taken that all the monks who had been approved by the council should be embarked for America; and if at the time of embarking any were wanting, they should be brought in and embarked with the rest. Nor should they be allowed to remain in the Canaries, if for any reason the vessels halted there on the outward passage; but from those islands no monk might go to America without the royal license. Generally, strangers, even when they held licenses from their superiors, were not permitted by the Casa de Contratacion to go to the Indies. Also monks not in obedience to their prelates were not passed, nor were those belonging to orders having no convents in the Indies. If any such should find their way to America, the governors of the ports of their landing were instructed to return them to Spain, unless they carried a special license from the king. A license to go to America served only for the first voyage. Having returned to Spain, one was not permitted to go a second time without a new license. If monks were sent to the Indies at the expense of the royal treasury, they were obliged to go to the places to which they had been assigned. And they

were held to this order, even though they returned to the royal treasury the amount that
had been advanced in their behalf. Those,
however, who wished to go to the Philippine
Islands were allowed to do so without hindrance; and by a law of 1572, the civil authorities were commanded to allow Jesuits bearing
licenses from their superiors to pass unhindered
from province to province, and they were to be
aided in accordance with their needs.[1]

Regarding the monasteries to be founded in
the Indian towns, the law provided that they
must be at least six leagues distant from one
another, and that the buildings should be plain
and of moderate size. In case the *encomiendas*
had been incorporated in the crown, the cost
of construction should be borne by the king;
but in case the *encomiendas* were held by private
persons, they should be built at the expense of
the king and the *encomenderos*, aided by the
Indians of the towns as they might be able.
Each monastery founded in the Indies with
the royal license and in new towns should be
provided out of the royal treasury with an
ornament, a chalice with its cover, and a bell.

Every three years the viceroys, presidents,
and governors were required to make a detailed
report concerning the monks in their respective
districts, and on the basis of these reports, the

[1] *Recop. de Indias*, Lib. i., Tit. xiv., Leyes 1–26.

king determined whether it was advisable or
not to send inspectors to the Indies. If sent,
they were to observe the state of the monks,
on what points reform was needed; they were
also required to avoid unnecessary disturbance,
and always aim at the perfection of the religious
life.[1]

The close union of civil and ecclesiastical
affairs is seen in the fact that the laws regulating both are brought together in a single code.
The *Recopilacion de Leyes de las Indias* contains
not only the purely political laws, but also
those regulating the conduct of the prebendaries
of the cathedral. The latter provided that the
prebendaries should reside in the churches to
which they belonged; that they should not
absent themselves from the services in which
they had been assigned parts; and that they
should not go out for visits or for any other
purpose, except under permission granted by
superior authority. The penalty for violation
of these regulations was a loss of office. Permission, in cases of great necessity, might be
granted by the prelate and the chapter; but
if the prelate and the chapter could not agree,
the viceroy, the president, or the governor
should unite with them to effect a decision.
The archbishops and bishops were required to
take such measures as would enforce, on the

---

[1] *Recop. de Indias*, Lib. i., Tit. xiv., Leyes 42–44.

part of the prebendaries, a complete fulfilment of their obligations, and to collect a fine in case of failure in this respect. The prelates, the viceroys, the presidents, and the governors were expected to make detailed reports to the king concerning the prebendaries; those actually in service, those who had died, and the existing vacancies and the causes of them. These civil officers were prohibited from granting licenses to go to Spain to the archbishops, bishops, or the holders of any other ecclesiastical office or benefice, the granting of such licenses being strictly reserved to the king.[1]

In relation to the conduct of affairs the clergy were subject to important limitations. No member of the clergy might be an alcalde, an advocate, or a notary, nor an agent of the *encomenderos*, or of any other person; neither were the clergy permitted to engage in any kind of business. They might not work mines, inasmuch as this, besides being unbecoming their positions, might result in a scandal or an evil example.[2]

According to a law of March 17, 1619, the parish priests were required to know the language of the Indians to whom they were appointed to carry the Christian doctrine; by a later law, however, they were ordered, in 1634, to take

[1] *Recop. de Indias*, Lib. i., Tit. xi.
[2] *Ibid.*, Tit. xii.

such measures " that all the Indians should be taught Spanish, and in this language the doctrines of Christianity, in order that they might the better comprehend the mysteries of the holy Catholic faith." [1]

Writing with copies of grants of *encomiendas* made by Pizarro before him, Prescott affirms that " they emphatically enjoin on the colonist the religious instruction of the natives under his care, as well as kind and considerate usage." That a certain course of action was enjoined by law is not all that is necessary to know in order to judge wisely of the conduct of the Spanish settlers towards the Indians. It is not safe to infer that in Spanish America the practice has been what the law implies it should have been. In this case an anonymous contemporary, apparently knowing how little attention was given to these pious instructions, states that " from this time forth the pest of personal servitude was established among the Indians, equally disastrous to body and soul of both the master and the slave." [2]

If we were to judge from the language of the laws of the Indies, we might conclude that the king, in dealing with the inhabitants, regarded no object as of more importance than their conversion to the Christian faith. His obliga-

[1] *Recop. de Indias*, Lib. i., Tit. xiii., Leyes 4 and 5.
[2] *Conquest of Peru*, ii., 37.

tions to seek this end he considered greater
than those of any other prince, as his dominions
were greater. In this view, he commanded
the officers of the crown in the several provinces
to make the Indians lay aside their savage
vices, and to instruct them in the holy Catholic
faith. He charged the archbishops and bishops
and other ecclesiastical officers to preach, teach,
and persuade the natives to accept the articles
of this faith. Through the law he commanded
the viceroys, the audiencias, and the governors
" to take very especial care to convert and
Christianize the Indians," and provided that
they should instruct them in the things of the
holy Catholic church and the evangelical law.
They should, moreover, aid in rooting out
idolatry among the Indians, destroying or
carrying off their idols, and preventing the natives under severe penalties from worshipping
them. Those among the Indians who taught
idolatry should be taken and distributed among
the convents, where they might be instructed
in the doctrines of the church. In each of the
Christian towns there should be indicated definite hours each day, in which all the Indians,
negroes, and mulattoes, the slaves as well as
those who were free, should be brought together to listen to Christian doctrine; and the
law required, furthermore, that these persons
should not be hindered or occupied with any-

17

thing else at the appointed hour. The negroes,
mulattoes, and Indians who lived outside of the
towns should be called together for the same
purpose when they came into the towns on
holidays. All persons who had slaves, either
negroes or mulattoes, should send them to the
church or monastery, at the hour which the
prelate might indicate, and they should there
be instructed in the principles of the Christian
faith ; the archbishops and bishops should have
specially in mind their conversion and instruction. On Sundays and feast days no one might
be hindered from going to the church or the
monastery to hear mass and receive Christian
instruction, not even the slave by his master.
The penalty for such interference was fixed at
two hundred thousand maravedis, one half of
which would go to the general treasury, and
the other half to the building of churches.
Whoever should have unconverted Indians in
his service, whether by the day or by the year,
should send them to church every morning ;
and in case one should not comply with this
requirement, he should be deprived of the service of the Indian or Indians concerned, who
would never be permitted to serve him again,
and he should, moreover, pay a fine of four
dollars for each day of his failure to comply
with the law, one half of which should go to
the *Confradia* of the Indians, and the other

half to the judge. On Sundays and other days when they were obliged to hear mass, the Indians, negroes, and mulattoes might not be compelled to work.[1]

In order that the natives of the Indies might have due reverence and respect for the churches, for the ecclesiastics, and for the holy sacraments and doctrines, the law imposed numerous restrictions on conduct in the churches, and provided that those should not be admitted who ought not to take advantage of the immunity which the sacred places afforded. The immunity of the church should not extend to soldiers and sailors who had passed to the Indies in the armadas or fleets, and had remained without license. Because their remaining was opposed to the public good, they might be taken from the churches, convents, or sacred places, and handed over to commanders of their vessels.

The power of the Inquisition was extended to Mexico at first through certain persons who acted as agents for this court. To this class belonged the Franciscan missionary, Valencia, and the superiors of the Dominican order. Later there were officially appointed inquisitors ; and towards the end of Archbishop Montúfar's administration the Inquisition, as a regularly organized tribunal, was established in

[1] *Recop. de Indias*, Lib. i., Tit. ii.

Mexico. This was in 1571; and Dr. Pedro de
Moya y Contreras, who later succeeded Montúfar as archbishop and then became viceroy,
was made the chief inquisitor. The first *auto-
de-fé* of Mexico was held in 1574, three years
after the introduction of the Inquisition into
that country.[1]

Owing to the great distances between the
residences of the bishops, and the great expenses that would be entailed by frequent as-
semblies, it was provided, in accordance with
the decision of Pope Paul V., that the provincial councils might be held at intervals of twelve
years. The viceroy, the president, or the
governor, each in his district, attended these
councils in the name of the king, and as the
king's representative. Synodical councils were
convoked in the archbishoprics and bishoprics
every year, and the archbishops and bishops
were charged to make these meetings as inex-
pensive as possible. The prelates were, moreover, required to allow the members of the
regular and secular clergy to vote freely at
these meetings, and to express their opinions
without hindrance. Measures were also taken
to prevent the publication of any conclusions,
by either council, adverse to the royal supremacy.[2]

[1] Torquemada, iii., 377.
[2] *Recop. de Indias*, Lib. i., Tit. viii.

There was observed at times a marked disposition on the part of the ecclesiastical courts to encroach upon the civil authority. In view of this, the audiencias were commanded to hold inviolable, in their districts, the royal jurisdiction. At the same time, the ecclesiastical judges were prohibited from taking cognizance of civil cases and also of criminal cases arising among those who had not accepted the Christian faith. Among other restrictions placed on the ecclesiastical judges we find them charged " not to condemn the Indians to labor, nor to permit them to be defrauded of their wages," nor for any cause whatsoever to condemn them to pecuniary punishments.[1]

Before the close of the sixteenth century much attention had been directed to the ecclesiastical organization of Peru. Bishops had been appointed, convents and religious fraternities had been established, every village had its parish priest, and the foundations of the Inquisition had been laid. The first archbishop of Lima, Geronimo de Loaysa, died in 1575, and was succeeded, after the see had been vacant for six years, by Dr. Toribio Mogrovejo, who undertook extensive missionary journeys throughout the kingdom. Through councils and synods he directed the organization of the church, and provided means for educating

---

[1] *Recop. de Indias*, Lib. i., Tit. x.

priests by founding the College of San Toribio.
To these early years belong the lives of at least
three Peruvian saints: San Toribio, Santa Rosa
de Lima, and San Francisco Solano.

CHAPTER XI

SPAIN'S ECONOMIC POLICY IN AMERICA

A FACT of great importance in revealing the economic characteristics of Spanish rule in America was, that discoveries and settlements were usually made, not at the expense of the state, but with private funds. If at any time the crown made advances for the support of an expedition, it was regarded as a loan to be repaid out of the first proceeds of the undertaking; and assurance was given that the settlements should remain under Spanish authority. A decree of Charles V., which has been incorporated in the laws of the Indies, affirms that in recognition of

"the fidelity of our vassals, and the pains which the discoverers and settlers experienced in their discoveries and settlements, and in order that they may have more certainty and confidence of these always remaining united to our Royal crown, we promise, and pledge our faith and royal word, in behalf of ourselves and the kings our successors forever, that their cities and settlements, on no account or reason, or in favor of any person whatever, shall be alienated or separated, wholly or in part ; and that if we or any of our successors should make any gift or alienation thereof, contrary to this express declaration, the same shall be held as null and void." [1]

However benevolent may have been the king's intentions which found expression in this decree, it is now clear that these intentions could not be carried out, that the sovereign of Spain could not bind his successors, and, moreover, that this pledge was later actually violated.

One of the earliest features of Spain's economic policy with reference to America was the adoption of the system of *encomiendas*. This system involved the granting of lands to Spanish subjects, together with authority to command the services of a certain number of Indians. The Indians were expected to cultivate the lands, and thus make them a source of income to those persons who had received them from the king. In the contemplation of the law, the Spanish settlers held Indians in service not merely for the profits of their labor, but also for the purpose of teaching them the Christian doctrine, and of defending their persons and property.

[1] *Recop. de Indias*, Lib. iii., Tit. i., Ley i.

Although this system placed the Indians in the position of serfs, the conduct of the Spaniards in this matter was not without its apologists. It was urged that the condition of the Indians was in some sense improved by the conquest; human sacrifices were abolished, and through the introduction of mules the Indians were released from at least a share of their oppressive and degrading occupations. " The Indians whose liberty had in vain been proclaimed by Queen Isabella, were till then slaves of the whites, who appropriated them to themselves indiscriminately. By the establishment of the *encomiendas*, slavery assumed a more regular form." [1]

The fundamental idea of the commercial and industrial policy of Spain, as carried out through the India House, was that of restriction and privilege. It involved the granting of exclusive privileges to certain persons or companies, and to certain ports; and it was expected by the holders of these privileges that the monopolies which they had received would continue to be maintained. But they found in the course of time that, by reason of the growth of contraband trade, they had to engage in sharp competition, and that, instead of being a source of profit, their undertakings threatened to lead to their ruin. With this prospect, the

[1] Humboldt, *New Spain*, i., 181.

companies sometimes made effort to induce
the government to compel their privileges to
be respected. To have enforced a strict ob-
servance of these privileges might have given
a temporary advantage to the holders of them,
but the colonists would have suffered in consequence.

While the trade with America was required
by law to pass through Porto Bello and Vera
Cruz, the southern part of the continent was
invaded by European wares through the contraband trade of Portugal. This and the subsequent concessions in favor of Buenos Aires
appear to have alarmed the monopolists of
Peru. Buenos Aires, which had hitherto been
a closed port, was permitted to receive two
small vessels from Spain, and the Peruvians
feared that the wares brought in these ships
and entered annually at the port of Buenos
Aires, would render unnecessary a resort to the
Peruvian markets, and that these wares would
be even carried across the continent, and introduced into Lima, thus violating the Peruvians'
exclusive control of the trade of the western
coast.[1] Against these concessions and the

---

[1] Don Jose de Armendaris, viceroy of Peru from 1724 to
1736, said : " Es Buenos Aires la ruina de los dos comercios,
la puerta por donde se le huye la riqueza, y la ventana por
donde se arroja el Peru. Es un lugar de encanto, donde un
real permiso se trasforma en una infiel usurpacion y donde aún

illicit trade of the Portuguese, Peru raised a vigorous protest. It was, moreover, a violation of the strictly protective system, under which Spanish America was held, that trade should be found following lines not marked out by the prescriptions of the law. To avoid these disapproved results, the Council of the Indies established a line of custom-houses in the interior of the continent, separating the provinces of La Plata from those of the Pacific. With no outlet for their products, the flocks and herds multiplied on the rich plains of Uruguay and Buenos Aires, and without a market they were without value.

In the trade in hides, under the limited privileges extended to the port of Buenos Aires, it was required that these hides should be of a certain size. But it happened that about three eighths of those secured by the method in vogue for slaughtering the animals were too small, and had to be rejected. Besides the hides, the only other portions of the animals then preserved were the tongue and the fat.[1] In the first half of the eighteenth century the

la plata inocente va culpada. Contra este fatal daño ha clamado siempre este comercio ; contra él se han expuesto los jueces y contra él han se agotado las providencias." See Pelliza, *Historia Argentina*, i., 91.

[1] Letter of F. Cajetan Cattaneo, dated Reduction of St. Mary, Paraguay, April 30, 1730, printed in Muratori's *Missions of Paraguay*, 250.

price of negroes at Buenos Aires was from one
hundred to two hundred dollars a piece.

The growth of Buenos Aires during the first
two decades after its re-establishment in 1580
was so slow that, in 1602, it contained not
more than five hundred inhabitants besides the
Indians and negro slaves. The increased freedom which the people of Buenos Aires obtained
in the course of time gave an important impulse
to progress in this province. Paraguay, on the
other hand, became isolated; the immigration
to this interior region was, in large part, inter-
cepted by Buenos Aires; and some portion of
the territory, in the hands of the Jesuits, felt
the paralyzing effect of ecclesiastical socialism.
Paraguay's long conflicts with Brazil still further
impeded her advance in material prosperity.
Progress in Buenos Aires, even if it outran that
of Paraguay, was hindered by the lack of effective incentives to immigration and enterprise.
When the Indians of Rio de la Plata were subdued and the lands explored, the Spaniards did
not turn with great enthusiasm from a life of
exciting adventure to the tame existence of a
farmer or a herdsman. To make the rich
plains of Buenos Aires give up their wealth
required persistent labor, but it was not for
this that the bulk of the Spaniards had sought
the New World. In the discovery and development of mines, as they were found in Mexico

and Peru, there was always an opportunity for
severe labor, but there was also the possibility
of great rewards. In carrying war into the
wilderness against the Indians, there were,
moreover, always difficulties and dangers, but
there was also the possibility of capturing a
prince, whose ransom might suddenly enrich
an army. Therefore, after the period of the adventurers was passed, and the affairs of the
province had assumed a settled order, Buenos
Aires was outrun by other colonies in the competition for settlers to aid in the development
of her resources.

If the material development of Buenos Aires
was rapid in comparison with the towns of
Paraguay, it was slow in comparison with the
growth of certain towns in the mining regions,
and this slowness was due in a large measure,
among other things, to the fact that Buenos
Aires had been a closed port. If later certain
concessions were made, favoring a limited
amount of direct trade with Spain, there was
revealed in this no intention to depart from the
general policy which had been adhered to previously. The concessions made in the first
half of the seventeenth century failed to satisfy
the inhabitants; for, while a certain amount of
freedom was granted on the east, trade with
Tucuman and Peru was cut off on the west,
except on the condition of paying a duty of

fifty per cent. This duty indicates that the Spanish administration had not departed from its restrictive policy, for the purpose of this duty was to increase the prices of goods imported to the western provinces by way of Buenos Aires, in order to make them equal to the prices of goods brought by the established route of Panama, and thus to prevent the shipments to Buenos Aires from interfering with the monopoly of Peru.[1]

An important feature of the trade with America was the traffic in slaves from Africa. Black slaves were introduced into Spain as early as 1442, and the modern trade in negroes began about that time. In the " year 1444, Europe may be said to have made a distinct beginning in the slave trade."[2] Slaves were first carried to the Spanish Islands in 1503.[3] Several negroes were conveyed to America as early as 1510. They were taken on the private account of King Ferdinand. But in 1516 the exclusive privilege to transport negroes to America was granted to a person named Chevris, who ceded this right to a company of Genoese merchants for the sum of 23,000 ducats. The first negroes dispatched under this privilege were one thousand sent to San

[1] Mitre, *Historia de Belgrano*, i., 33.
[2] Helps, *Spanish Conquest*, i., 51.
[3] Pradt, *The Colonies*, 80.

Domingo, in 1517.[1] After the recommendation of Las Casas concerning the importation
of negro slaves had been adopted, it was thought
that four thousand would be adequate to meet
the immediate demands. By the *asiento* of
1517, Charles V. extended the privilege of this
trade to De Dresa, a Fleming, under the assurance of a monopoly for eight years, which had
the effect of increasing the price of negroes.
In the last years of the sixteenth century, Philip
II. had great need of money, and he sought to
procure it by granting for a consideration the
exclusive privilege of the slave trade with
America. Gomez Reinel held this privilege
from 1595 to 1600, when it was granted to a
Portuguese named Juan Rodriguez Contineo,
who argeed to furnish to the Indies annually
4250 slaves, and to pay to the crown 160,000
ducats. On the death of Rodriguez Contineo,
his privilege and obligations under this contract
fell to his brother, and at the time of the transfer the annual payment to the crown was reduced 22,000 ducats. A few years later, in
1615, the *asiento* was granted to Antonio Fer-
nandez Delvas, for the period of eight years.
Delvas was a Portuguese, and under his contract he was obliged to introduce into America
each year 3500 slaves, and to pay 115,000
ducats to the crown. At the expiration of the

[1] *Present State of Peru*, 89.

period of this grant, the *asiento* was assigned
for another eight years to another Portuguese,
Manuel Rodriguez Lamego, who agreed to
introduce the same number of slaves, 3500,
but to increase by 5000 ducats the annual payment. During the eight years following 1631,
the contract called for a payment to the crown
of 95,000 ducats, and the introduction of 2500
slaves. After this period there was an inter-
ruption of this form of the slave trade till 1662.
In this year the *asiento* was granted to Domingo
Grillo and Ambrosio Lomelin, for a term of
seven years, during which they were required
to introduce 24,500 negroes, and pay the king
2,100,000 dollars. In 1674, the privilege of
this trade passed to Antonio Garcia and Sebastian de Siliceo, who were required to import
annually 4000 slaves, and pay 450,000 dollars.
Owing to a failure on the part of this company
to comply with the terms of the grant, it was
recalled in 1676, and conferred on a company
in Seville. In 1682, the privilege of this trade
was granted for five years to Juan Barroso del
Pozo and Nicolas Porcio, residents of Cadiz.
They had agreed to pay 1,125,000 dollars, but,
as they failed in this, the contract was transferred to a Hollander, Baltasar Coimans. Prior
to this time the holders of this privilege had
been Europeans, but in 1692 it was assigned to
Bernardo Francisco Martin de Guzman, **of**

Venezuela, for five years, on the payment of 2,125,000 dollars. He was followed, in 1696, by the Portuguese Company of Guinea, who held the *asiento* for six years, after which it passed to the French Guinea Company, and finally, by the treaty of 1713, the monopoly of the slave trade with Spanish America fell into the hands of the English.[1]

Under the *asiento* of 1713, an English company was obliged to introduce 144,000 negroes into Spanish America, within thirty years, beginning May 1, 1713, at the rate of 4800 each year. For each negro the company was required to pay thirty-three dollars and a third, which would cover all duties that existed then or that might be imposed later. The company was required, moreover, to advance to the Spanish king 200,000 dollars in two equal payments, the first to be made two months after the signing of the contract, and the second two months after the first. This amount was not to be returned to it till after twenty years; then for the last ten years of the specified term it might withhold 20,000 dollars a year from the duties otherwise payable. In consideration

[1] Calvo, *Coleccion Completa de los Tratados de la America Latina*, ii., 53–55 ; for the *Asiento* of 1696, see pp. 5–42 ; for that of 1701, see pp. 60–77 ; for that of 1713, see pp. 78–101 ; also *The Asiento ; or Contract for Allowing to the Subjects of Great Britain the Liberty of Importing Negroes into the Spanish America*, printed by John Baskett. London, 1713.

of the advance payment of 200,000 dollars, the risks, and the interest, the company was required to pay duty on only 4000 negroes annually, the remaining 800 being admitted without payment. The importation in any given year was, however, not limited to the prescribed 4800. There was, in fact, an inducement offered to have it exceed that number; for each negro imported over that number in the first twenty-five years of the term, there was required a duty of only sixteen dollars and two thirds.

For carrying on this trade, the company might employ either British or Spanish ships. In case Spanish ships were used, it must be with the consent of their owners, freight being paid them. The ships, moreover, might be manned with either English or Spanish sailors. In view of the fact that those provinces which had not had landing-places for slaves hitherto, had been considered as enduring great hardships, it was by this contract provided that negroes might be sold in all ports of the Atlantic where there were royal officers to certify to the number imported. At the same time three hundred dollars was fixed as the maximum price for which negroes might be sold in the ports of Santa Marta, Cumana, and Maracaybo, but in the ports of Mexico and Central America, the company might sell them for whatever it might be able to get for them. Of the annual importation of 4800 negroes, 1200 might be taken to the Rio de la Plata, 800 for Buenos Aires, and 400 for neighboring provinces, and there sold without restriction as to price. On the Pacific coast of South America, only the ports of Peru were open to the company. To these it was permitted to ship negroes from Panama, and to enter at Panama without duty the gold and silver brought back as the produce of their sales. This trade enjoyed other exemptions from the established duties. Whatever cables, sails, iron, or other stores and provisions were necessary for the ships engaged in the trade between Panama and Peru might be entered at Porto Bello without duty, but the articles so entered might not be sold. For the management of the trade in negroes, the company was permitted to employ either English or Spanish,

" his Catholic majesty dispensing for that end, with the laws which forbid strangers entering into or inhabiting that country; declaring and commanding that the English, during the whole time of this *asiento*, shall be regarded and treated as if they were subjects of the crown of Spain, with this restriction, that there shall not reside in any one of the said ports of the Indies more than four or six Englishmen." [1]

[1] *The Asiento ; or Contract for Allowing to the Subjects*

For the administration of its affairs, the company was empowered to appoint " in all the ports and chief places of America, Judges Conservators of this *asiento* whom it may remove and displace, and appoint others at pleasure." For their removal, however, it was necessary to show cause that would be approved by the president, governor, or audiencia of the district. These judges were to have exclusive jurisdiction in all cases relating to the *asiento*, and the authorities of the country, even the viceroys, were forbidden to interfere. But from the decisions of these judges appeals might be taken to the Council of the Indies.

The royal officers might not lay an embargo on the ships of the company, or detain them for any cause whatsoever; but they were " obliged to afford them all favor, assistance, and succor"; nor could they under any pretence seize their stock, goods, or effects, or search their warehouses, except after proved fraudulent importation, and then only with the assistance of a judge conservator. In shipping their goods to Europe the company was permitted to make use of Spanish vessels, by " agreeing for the freight with the captains and owners of

of Great Britain the Liberty of Importing Negroes into the Spanish America, Art. xi., printed by John Baskett. London, 1713.

the ships "; or it might employ its own vessels under the free convoy of the Spanish ships of war. And all goods thus imported into Spain would be admitted free of duty, the stock of the company being regarded as having " the same privilege as if it belonged to his Catholic majesty."

The formation of this contract made it unlawful " for the French Guinea Company or for any other person whatsoever to introduce any negro slave into India," under penalty of confiscation of ships and negroes. The ships engaged in the trade in negroes under this contract might not be used for taking to Spain either Spanish passengers or goods belonging to Spanish subjects; and on arriving at American ports they should be " searched to the bottom, even to the ballast," and any goods found on board should be seized and the guilty parties punished. But provisions put on shore to maintain the negroes should be exempt from duty. In case, however, more were landed than could be consumed, the surplus might be sold after paying the duties established at the port in question. The duties on negroes imported were due as soon as the arrangements preparatory to landing had been made by the royal officers. If any of the negroes should die before they were sold, this fact would not exempt them from duty, except in cases where they were found to be ill, and were landed not for sale but for the sake of improving their health, and should die within fifteen days after landing. If they were alive at the expiration of fifteen days, they would be subject to duty. Having paid duty at one port, negroes might be transported to another port, and entered without payment, on the presentation of the proper certificate from the officers of the first port.

This contract was not formed without regard to the revenues of the kings of England and Spain.

" It is agreed and stipulated that both their majesties shall be concerned for one half of this trade, each of them a quarter part which shall belong to him, pursuant to this agreement. And whereas it is necessary that his Catholic majesty, in order to have and enjoy the benefit and gain that may be obtained by this trade, should advance to the said company one million dollars, or a quarter of the sum which shall be judged necessary for the putting of this commerce into a good order and method, it is agreed and settled that if his Catholic majesty shall not think it convenient to advance the said sum, the aforementioned *asientists* do offer to do it out of their own money, upon condition that his Catholic majesty shall make good the interest out of what they shall be accountable for to him, at the rate of eight per cent. yearly.''

At the end of the first five years, the company was required to render to the king of Spain a sworn account

" of the charge of the purchase, subsistence, and sale of the negroes, and all other expenses upon their account; and also certificates in due form, of the produce of their sale in all ports and parts of America belonging to his Catholic majesty, whither they shall have been imported and sold; which accounts, as well of the charge as of the produce, are first to be examined and settled by her Britanic majesty's ministers employed in this Service, in regard to the share she is to have in this *asiento*, and then to be examined in like manner by this court; and his Catholic majesty's share of the profits may be adjusted and recovered from the *asientists*, who are to be obliged to pay the same most regularly and punctually, in pursuance of this article."

Out of the profits of the first five years the company might reimburse itself for the advance of the Spanish king's quarter part and for the interest. A similar account was required every five years successively. For three years after the expiration of the thirty years specified in the contract, the company should enjoy the same privileges and immunities as were guaranteed to it for the term of the contract, in order to give it opportunity " to adjust its accounts, and gather in all its effects in the Indies, and to make up a balance of the whole." A special provision was made for collecting debts due the company, by placing them on the same footing as debts due the king.

The participation of Spain in the affairs covered by this contract was through a committee of three appointed by the king from the Council of the Indies. In case of war between Spain and England, the company should have a year and a half to withdraw its effects from Spain and the Indies; but in case of war between either of these kingdoms and another nation, the ships belonging to the company should be neutral and carry passes and special colors. For the thirty years of the contract and three additional years, all Spanish laws in conflict with the terms of this agreement were set aside in favor of the contract. And whatever liberties, favors, privileges, and exemptions had been granted to any former company were turned to the advantage of the company under this contract, in so far as they were not in conflict with any of its specific provisions. In addition to the trade in negroes, the company was permitted to participate in the general trade with the Indies to the extent of the capacity of one ship of five hundred tons a year during the specified thirty years. In this trade the king of Spain was to have one-fourth

interest, and to receive five per cent. of the
net gain of the other three fourths.   The goods
imported into America under this provision
were to be exempt from duty, and could be
sold only at the fair of Porto Bello.   If the
vessel carrying them should arrive before the
Spanish fleet, they were to be stored in warehouses locked with two keys, one of which
should be held by the royal officers of the port,
and the other by the agents of the company.

   The articles of the treaty of 1713, which referred to the participation of the English in the
annual fair at Porto Bello, were explained and
modified by a subsequent treaty made in 1716.
The English had complained, that on account
of irregularity as to time and place of holding
the fair and of the difficulty of preserving their
wares, particularly at Porto Bello, the trade
was likely to be attended with loss rather than
gain.   In this treaty the king of Spain agreed
" to inform the English court of the exact
time of the sailing of the Spanish vessels for
the Indies, so that the company might cause
its ship to sail at the same time."   In case the
Spanish vessels should not leave Cadiz in the
month of June, the English company might
send its vessel, having informed the Spanish
government of the time of its departure.   If it
arrived at the port where it had been determined to hold the fair, at Cartagena, Porto

Bello, or Vera Cruz, before the arrival of the
Spanish vessels, it should wait for them four
months, after which its wares might be sold
without restriction.

This treaty contained another concession to
the English company. It was found that sometimes more wares were taken to Africa for the
purchase of slaves than could be used. In
such cases, as there were no warehouses in
Africa, the company wished the privilege of
transporting the surplus to the Indies. The
king of Spain acceded to this wish with respect to Buenos Aires, because " between
Africa and the port of Buenos Aires there was
no island or landing-place under the British king
where the vessels of the *asiento de negros* could
halt." This was not true of the ports of Caracas, Cartagena, Porto Bello, Vera Cruz, Havana,
Porto Rico, and San Domingo; for Jamaica and
other islands of the West Indies were already
under British authority, and furnished as accessible harbors as those under the control of the
Spaniards. It was, moreover, determined to
make the term of the *asiento* begin on the first
of May, 1714, instead of one year earlier, as had
been provided in the treaty of 1713, and to have
the terms of the payments arranged accordingly.[1]

[1] Tractado declaratorio de algunos articulos del asiento de
negros que se pacto el 26 de marzo de 1716 con la Inglaterra,
concluido en Madrid el 26 de mayo de 1716. This treaty is
printed in Calvo's *Coleccion*, ii., 181–186.

Under this treaty the English had been granted the privilege of participating in the trade of the Indies to the extent of the wares that might be carried in one ship of five hundred tons sailing annually. In order to derive from this concession the maximum advantage the representatives of this thrifty nation took with their privileged ship sometimes five or six smaller vessels loaded with goods. When they arrived near Porto Bello, the provisions and furniture were removed from the privileged vessel, and she was filled to the rigging with wares taken from the little ships in attendance. By this simple artifice the privileged ship was made to carry more than five or six of the largest ships of Spain. The English being able to sell cheaper than the Spaniards, that indulgence, according to the Spanish view, "was of infinite detriment to the commerce of Spain." [1] After this first invasion of Spain's exclusive control, that country appeared unable to furnish the goods that were demanded by her transatlantic possessions, and their wants had to be supplied from other countries. Holland followed England, and in the course of time every manufacturing nation of Europe had part in the trade with Spanish America.

To surround the violation of commercial regulations with all the terrors of the law, it

[1] Ulloa, *A Voyage to South America*, i., 106.

was provided that in case foreigners should succeed in entering Spanish-American ports, the inhabitants should not trade with them, on pain of death and confiscation of property. But these laws were not effective. The number of foreigners in the seaport towns and the amount of foreign trade increased, and in certain quarters, particularly at Buenos Aires, the contraband trade very early exceeded the legal trade with Spain. In fact, the city of Buenos Aires outran in its growth other towns because of the great advantages of the contraband trade over the legitimate trade.

Not only in commerce but also in agriculture was the Spanish policy restrictive. As late as 1803, " orders were received in Spanish America from Spain to root up all the vines in certain provinces, because the Cadiz merchants complained of a diminution in the consumption of Spanish wines." [1]　Spain objected also to the cultivation of tobacco in Spanish America, and the inhabitants were prevented from raising flax, hemp, or saffron. The cultivation of the olive was forbidden, lest it might limit the market for Spanish oil. If in Buenos Aires the inhabitants were allowed to cultivate grapes and olives, it was only " by special permission, and only in sufficient quantity for the table."

The Spanish policy with reference to the

---

[1] Hall, *Journal*, i., 296.

American possessions not only imposed restrictions on industry and commerce, but also on the movement of population. The violation of laws concerning this latter subject was punished with confiscation of property, one fourth of which went to the informer, and the rest to the royal treasury. Although the policy respecting migration reveals a vicious tendency to hedge about a popular movement with too many restrictions, it must be admitted that some of the regulations indicate a humane spirit on the part of the makers of the law. Such was the requirement that no slave who was married should be allowed to go to the Indies without his wife and children. The restrictions on emigration necessitated a slow increase in the population of the Spanish colonies, and thus permitted a more complete assimilation of the Spaniard to the Indian type than would have been possible had the emigration to the colonies been unrestrained and rapid.

But the people of Spanish America complained that the restrictions which were imposed upon them sacrificed the well-being of a continent to the ignorance and selfishness of the Spanish court and its privileged adherents. If a settler on the bank of the Rio de la Plata wished some article of European production, for a long time the route by which it could reach him in the course of legitimate trade was from Seville to Porto Bello, from Porto Bello across the Isthmus to Panama, from Panama to Lima, and from Lima across the continent to its destination. The effect of this, except in a few favored places, like Lima and the City of Mexico, was to prevent the use of European wares, and to compel the settlers to accept such substitutes as they were able to produce or obtain from the Indians. In other words, the trade restrictions which were imposed upon the colonies, instead of permitting them to start with the advantages of the achievements of European civilization, in many cases drove them back to the barbarism of the aborigines, and doomed them to go over again the painful way up to civilization, which their ancestors had trod in Europe. To go from Spain to America, except to a few privileged places, was not merely to go into exile, but even to renounce civilization. And not only this, for by reason of the restrictions placed on agriculture and the industries, as well as on trade, one was not given a free hand with which to work his way forward. It is true, there were no legal hindrances to the raising of cattle on the vast and fertile plains of the Argentine. But the natural ports of this region were closed, and there was no outlet towards the civilized world for the products of these ranges, except across

the continent to Peru, over the Isthmus to
Porto Bello, and from Porto Bello to Spain
once a year. With a limited population and
no exit, and with practically unlimited herds,
the value of these herds disappeared. In the
early years of the eighteenth century, even
after the port of Buenos Aires had been opened
to the extent of admitting two small vessels
annually, an ox was worth $1, a sheep from 3
to 4 cents, and a mare 10 cents. The prices
had risen to this amount from a still lower
point under the influence of the demand made
by these vessels for hides, strengthened by the
larger demand of the contraband trade of the
English and Portuguese. It was clear enough
to the people of the Argentine that to them a
closed port meant poverty, and a free port
prosperity. Their opposition to the Spanish
policy, and, in fact, to the Spanish rule, which
appeared in the beginning of this century, was
no sentimental opposition, but rested on the
hard basis of economical considerations. As
economical considerations were conspicuous in
the motives of the Dutch in revolting against
the authority of Spain, and furnished also an
important ground of the action which the thirteen English colonies took against the mother
country, so the industrial and commercial
restraints, with which Spain hampered the
economical development of South America,

constituted a standing grievance, and had great weight in ultimately determining the people to make themselves free. The intensity of the evils of restriction was decreased in the course of time, but for this no thanks were due to the authorities of Spain. The Spanish policy failed, because it involved an irrational scheme. It failed, because it undertook permanently to contravene the normal operation of economic forces. It broke of its own weight, and it left the people to whom it had applied with a weakened sense of their obligations to uphold the law.

The inhabitants of Spanish America, with unimportant exceptions, revolted against the protective system which had been imposed upon them. Prominent among the exceptions were the little towns of Panama and Porto Bello. As long as all trade to the greater part of South America had to pass the Isthmus, these ports, as points for the collection and distribution of the wares involved, maintained a degree of relative importance. They were naturally interested in the continuance of the royal policy. But the great bulk of the people desired freedom. They saw that governmental restrictions on trade were likely to be made in the interests of a few persons, or of certain limited sections. Buenos Aires, standing on the Atlantic shore facing Europe, objected to being made by law the extreme frontier, and the insignificant concession of 1618, which permitted two ships of 100 tons each to enter the port annually, failed to satisfy their commercial ambition. The inhabitants of this and other isolated provinces recognized that the commercial regulations violated their interests, and they were driven to decide between upholding a law which sacrificed their well-being, and giving countenance to a violation of this law, through which would come prosperity and progress. The result here was what might have been expected. The vast extent of the border of Spain's possessions made it impossible for her to guard it efficiently. Smuggling could therefore be carried on with impunity, and the high prices which had been given to European wares in America by the system of restriction, constituted a sufficient inducement to lead the merchants of other nations to engage in contraband trade.

The restrictive policy as it was carried out through the India House did not realize the magnificent expectations of Spain. At this time Spain had clearly the position of supreme advantage in the world. She was the leading power in Europe, and she owned the larger and better half of this continent. But under the influence of a policy of commercial jealousy, " her population declined, her manufactories

19

were ruined, her merchant marine ceased to
exist except in name, her capital was diminished, foreigners carried on her commerce by
means of contraband, and all the gold and
silver of the New World found their way to
other countries than Spain." [1]

But when the opportunities of two centuries
had been thrown away, the king of Spain was
compelled to acknowledge that the system
which had been wrought out with such aston-
ishing care and diligence, and upheld by a
marvellous administration, was a disappoint-
ment and a failure. He accepted the actual
condition of things into which the trade with
America had drifted in spite of the law, and
even extended the privileges of trade to ports
which had hitherto been closed. In 1764,
ships for America were allowed to depart from
Corunna for all the principal ports of the
Spanish colonies, and to return thither with
their cargoes of colonial produce. Ten years
later, in 1774, the several Spanish colonies were
permitted to trade with one another. In 1778,
there was promulgated a new commercial code
for the Indies, which enlarged the freedom of
trade between Spain and her American possessions, but did not extend this freedom to other
nations. According to the king's view, as expressed in the introduction to this law, to grant

[1] Mitre, *Belgrano*, i., 23.

freedom was the only means of re-establishing in their ancient vigor the agriculture, industry, and population of his dominions. Moved by this consideration, he opened various ports of Spain to the American trade, and a little later, in February, 1778, made concessions to the provinces of Buenos Aires, and to the kingdoms of Chile and Peru. Finally, in October of this year, the new code was established, and it was provided that it should contain all the points of the earlier concessions which had not been revoked.

Ships engaged in this trade had to belong entirely to the king's subjects, and be manned by sailors, two thirds of whom at least were Spaniards either by birth or naturalization. And all the principal ports both in Spain and Spanish America were open to this trade.

Although this law professes to establish "the free commerce of Spain with the Indies," the term here involved is not to be taken in the sense which attaches to it in current discussion. Ships might not sail without a license, and the wares which they carried were not all exempt from the payment of duties, although the duties when imposed were low, and varied according to the importance of the port of destination. Shipments to the smaller ports paid one and one half per cent. on goods produced by Spaniards, and four per cent. on all foreign manufactures, besides the amounts these may have paid on their introduction into Spain. Goods shipped to the more important ports paid three per cent., if they were Spanish products, and seven per cent., if produced in other countries, unless entirely exempt from duty. For a period of ten years Spanish manufactures of wool, and cotton, and certain other articles were admitted without payment. Notwithstanding these merely nominal duties, the new commercial code was essentially a code of freedom. It was a violation of the fundamental features of Spain's traditional policy; but it was for the advantage of both Spain and Spanish America. It called into action creative forces that had slept for centuries, and it gave indications of the beginning of a new economic life. But relief through freedom came too late. By centuries of unreasonable discrimination and unjust restriction, Spain had forfeited her parental rights ; and emancipation was the logical and inevitable step forward.

CHAPTER XII

SPANISH AND ENGLISH COLONIES IN AMERICA

THE peculiarities of the institutions of different nations are attributable in part to unlike climatic and geographical conditions, and in part to different race characteristics. The contrast between the political characteristics of France and Germany is to be attributed only in a very slight degree to geographical contrasts, but in a very large measure, immediately, to the inherited qualities of the inhabitants. But the differences between England and Germany, or between England and France, have been produced to a much greater extent by the force of different geographical conditions. Although at different epochs of English history political liberty has been temporarily suppressed, still the eclipse has been only partial and of a comparatively short duration. But in other countries, as in Spain, France,

Germany, with apparently favorable beginnings, the people early lost a share of their
ancient liberties. The superiority of England's
good fortune in this regard is largely due to
the geographical fact that it is an island. The
people from the continent, who settled England, brought with them no political wisdom
greater than that which they left behind with
their kindred. In their new home, however,
they found conditions favorable to the growth
of independence. Their circumstances here
favored the development of that political
wisdom which they had in common with the
whole Germanic people, and enabled the nation
to realize this wisdom in free institutions.

The fact that one nation has a different heritage from another to transmit may be due to
the influence of geographical conditions; yet
certain things in a nation's character we recognize as the immediate result of heredity. Even
if we are not disposed to accept this idea with
all the consequences that have been assigned
to it, yet there are undeniably certain characteristics which pass by inheritance from one
generation to another. There is no doubt that
the persistence of a national or race character
may be explained, to a certain extent, by the
fact of imitation, but, at the same time, there
survives by inheritance, in the nation as well as
in the individual man, somewhat that can be

accounted for neither on the ground of imitation nor on the ground of previous instruction.
There exists an inherited bias, aptitude, or
propensity, which makes certain ideas acceptable, and others repugnant, and will, therefore,
be likely to insure the adoption of the one and
the rejection of the other.

The fundamental similarity of the governments of all the nations of one race can be fully
explained only by taking account of a common
inheritance of primitive political traditions.
All the modern Aryan nations have governments organized on a common fundamental
plan, and this plan embraces the essential
features of the primitive government of the
stock from which these nations are descended.
This similarity may be explained as an inheritance by tradition, or as an inherited habit of
mind, which leads it to seek instinctively to
reproduce the primitive form of organizations.
For the light it throws not only on the form of
government, but also on its action, it is important to know the course of historical events
which have marked the nation's progress.   If
we would get a key to a nation's colonial policy,
we must know not only the form of its government, but also on what particular element in
the government stress has come to be laid.
With the retention of the three agencies of
power, there may still be only one of them

effective.   Spain retained her council and cortes
after she had become practically an absolute
monarchy.   England retains her crown and
Lords after she has drifted far towards democracy.   It is necessary to know not only
these things, but also the character of a nation's system of administration.   In the difference between Spain's system of centralized
administration and England's strong local government may be discovered the main explana-
tion of the difference between the institutions
which England and Spain planted in the New
World.

No ideas of governmental organization are
so familiar to colonists, or so likely to be carried
out, as those which have been realized in the
mother country.   Each state is likely to reproduce itself, with variations, in its colonies.
The method and spirit are transmitted, and
whatever variation in form appears is due to
the peculiar circumstances of the new settlement.

The colonies of Spain and England stand in
sharp contrast in this regard.   A Spanish
colony, whether viewed with reference to its
organization or to its influence, is widely different from an English colony.   The difference is
not merely casual; it is fundamental.   With
certain variations, it is the distinction which
existed between the colonies of the Greeks and

the Romans. The Greek settlements, made up of the voluntary overflow of the population of the mother country, were usually independent from the start.

" The migrations of the colonists were commonly undertaken with the approbation and encouragement of the states from which they issued ; and it frequently happened that the motive of the expedition was one, in which the interest of the mother country was mainly concerned ; as when the object was to relieve it of superfluous hands, or of discontented and turbulent spirits. But it was seldom that the parent state looked forward to any more remote advantage from the colony, or that the colony expected or desired any from the parent state. There was in most cases nothing to suggest the feeling of dependence on the one side, or a claim of authority on the other. The sons, when they left their homes to shift for themselves on a foreign shore, carried with them only the blessing of their fathers, and felt themselves completely emancipated from their control. Often the colony became more powerful than its parent, and the distance between them was generally so great as to preclude all attempts to enforce submission." [1]

The only bond between them was a moral sentiment growing out of the fact of a common origin.

[1] Thirlwall, *History of Greece*, ch. xii. (ii., 97).

The Roman colonies, on the other hand, formed a part of an elaborate scheme for extending Roman dominion. They were the creatures of the central power, and the main instruments for confirming its conquests. " The Grecian colonies were not intended to increase the power of the parent state by enlarging its dominions, and they were usually established in some unoccupied or partially occupied territory." But the Roman colonies were often

" established in existing towns, the citizens of which were ejected and deprived of their lands. . . . Instead of being independent of the parent state, they were strictly dependent on it, and the political rights of the colonists were very limited In fact, the Roman colonies were, in their origin, little more than garrisons in conquered fortified places, where land was allotted to the soldiers instead of pay and provisions." [1]

In the methods of their establishment, the English colonies were like the colonies of Greece. The colonies of Spain, although the funds for their original settlement were largely private, were, like the Roman colonies, creations of the central political organization, and were upheld and controlled by a power outside of themselves. Most English colonial dependencies have worked their way to prominence

[1] Lewis, *Government of Dependencies*, 116.

through a struggling age of feebleness. The Spanish dependencies, on the other hand, have from the outset been equipped with ample legal machinery. In theory all the vast possessions of Spain in America were dependencies of the crown, and not subject to the government of the authorities, aside from the king, that ruled in Spain. The English colonies could pretend to no such position.

"The leaders who conducted the various Spanish expeditions, the viceroys and governors who presided over the several colonies, the officers of justice, and the ministers of religion, were all appointed by the king's authority, and removable at his pleasure. The people who composed the new settlements were entitled to no privileges independent of the sovereign, or that served as a barrier against the crown."

The power that was exercised by the elected magistrates in the towns, was merely municipal, and was confined to their own interior commerce and police. All political power "centred in the crown, and in the officers of its nomination."

But the independent feebleness of the English settlement was more conducive to healthy social growth than the rigid and powerful rule of the Spanish royal officials. The knowledge of the viceroy's power and of his uncompromis-

ing jealousy of any interference in affairs falling
within the sphere of his prerogative paralyzed
all efforts of local self-help; and yet, by reason
of the multiplicity of his duties and the vast-
ness of his dominions and the indifference of
his subordinates, he could render no efficient
force to stimulate social action, and stagnation
therefore necessarily ensued.

The English settlement, beginning with the
town meeting as the only organization and
source of public authority, or rather of the
authority that was felt in the ordinary con-
cerns of life, grew by the internal forces of
an independent community, and acquired wisdom for social control by the slow and ex-
pensive process of experience. But however
unlike were the English and Spanish dependencies with respect to their social and political
institutions, there were certain fundamental
motives to their establishment, which were
the same for both. They were both under
the theories of wealth that then dominated the
world. They both sought gold and silver.
Spain sought them directly; England, under
the influence of the East India Company, in a
more roundabout way. Mexico and Peru furnished these metals directly from their mines,
and for this reason were regarded by Spain as
the most desirable possessions conceivable. No
effort was spared that might be necessary to

conquer and hold them. They contained in abundance what all nations looked upon as the basis of material salvation.

While Spain sought gold directly and made laws to prevent its exportation, England was willing under certain circumstances to allow it to leave the country. But the general ultimate aim of the English was the same as that of the Spaniards. If gold was allowed by the English to go out for raw material, it was in order that the raw material when elaborated might go out for a larger quantity of gold. There were, of course, colonies planted from other motives, like the Pilgrims on the shore of New England, but they did not represent the colonial policy of England.

From another point of view, the English and Spanish policies with reference to colonial dependencies have been somewhat wide apart. While Spain was sending Christian missionaries to extend the kingdom of heaven on earth, England was making some of her colonies, at least, places of banishment for her convicts. There is no doubt that one of the strongest motives of Spain's action was a genuine and honest desire for the spiritual regeneration of the native population, and that this desire was felt by many of those who sought to make themselves the instruments of this regeneration. But, at the same time, it will probably be acknowledged that ecclesiastics, when they have constituted the dominant factor, have not always furnished a hopeful basis for a new social organism. Where, as in Paraguay, the priest was for a time completely dominant, it may be said that the natives learned the arts of peace and were well started on the way towards civilized life. Yet the method of building up a society which had been adopted in the missions of South America had to undergo a revolution before any real progress could become possible. And the missions of California, when they were secularized, had gone about as far as it was possible to go on that line towards civilization. A few thousand natives had been reduced to a slave-like submission, and a few thousand cattle had been scattered over the hills and along the valleys, and at this point social progress had stopped.

But the most significant contrast between Spanish and English institutions in America appears with reference to the extent of power exercised in matters of local control. It is a contrast not only in methods of government, but also in means of political education. Under the rigid rule of the Council of the Indies and its subordinates, the great body of the people in the Spanish colonies learned only one lesson, and that was the necessity of obedience. The power of self-direction or self-control they had no opportunity to acquire. They only learned to follow; not because they saw any reason for going in one direction rather than in another, but because they were dominated by a superstition or habit favoring obedience, born of long subjection to absolute rule, and of inexperience in matters of public concern. The result of this was to make possible quiet and orderly conduct, as long as the power of the parent state remained unshaken; but it did not prepare the way for independent national action. When, therefore, the tie of allegiance to Spain was severed, the communities were like a ship without a rudder or ballast. There were no points of advantage that could be used to give them consistent movement in any direction. They were subject to the shifting currents of uninstructed prejudice. While the bulk of the people were willing to render obedience, they were without the means of determining to whom it should be rendered. They were perfect material for the demagogue, or the pliant tools of revolutionists. The Spanish-American attempts at self-government have, therefore, in most cases had a sorry outcome; not because of any original incapacity in the stock, but because of the lamentable political education which the dependencies received during their three centuries of bondage to Spain.

It is natural to cast the blame for the political shortcomings of Mexico and the South American republics on the republican scheme of government. The wonder, the rather, is that the republican system has been able to find here any tolerable application. Most of the evils which are charged against republicanism as a system of government, whether in the former Spanish dependencies of America, or in the now independent English settlements, cannot with justice be ascribed to republicanism, but are rather attributable to the unfortunate political antecedents of those who are attempting to live by the republican rule. The sins of the fathers are being visited upon the children. Previous education under monarchy is one of the chief sources of embarrassment to republican government. But the English colonies have been less unfortunate than the Spanish. Deriving from their mother country the spirit of liberty and local independence, their institutions have grown in harmony with their society. The zeal for political freedom which was manifest in a large part of the English nation, in the seventeenth century, and the ample provisions for self-government which had already been carried out by the English people, descended as a beneficent heritage upon the colonies of the English stock. On the other hand, the colonization of Mexico and South

America took place at a time when the ancient popular liberty of Spain had been suppressed, and the nation subjected to the despotic rule of the crown. The contrast between the origin of the Spanish-American states and that of the United States not only helps to explain the difference between their institutions, but also affords certain indications as to the difference between their later courses of political development. The settlers of the United States came from a nation which had resisted the encroachments of the crown; the settlers of Spanish America came from a country where the national parliament had already lost its power, and the government been removed from popular control. The Spanish settlers of Mexico and South America were, politically, representatives of a retrograde movement. Spain gave to her American possessions an inheritance of absolutism, in which the principle of liberty found little recognition. The traditions with which Spanish America began her career were the traditions of despotism, and any permanent advance towards liberty had to be made in opposition to these traditions. In the United States, on the contrary, the liberty of the people grew naturally out of their political traditions.

The institutions and practice of the English and Spanish colonies, when observed from

20

another point of view, present another important contrast. The United States were settled
by a people who, throughout a most remarkable career of conquest and colonization, have
never truckled to the savage, nor, for the sake
of influence over inferior races, been willing to
give up the purity of their blood. Since the
days of migration from the lowlands of Sles-
wick, the English people, in England, in
America, and in Australia, have moved stead-
ily and irresistibly forward, and their advance
has been marked by the disappearance of the
uncultivated aborigines. The English in colo-
nizing among ruder peoples have been uncompromising. To the barbarians whose territory
they have overrun, they have held out two
simple alternatives: either to accept the English standard of civilization, or to fold their
tents and depart. The Spaniards, on the other
hand, wherever they have met the native tribes
of America, have been willing to descend from
their European standard of civilization and
affiliate with them on a lower plane. In Spanish America, the Spaniards have mingled their
blood with the blood of the natives, and have
compromised with them in the formation of
political and religious institutions. The English policy has tended to exterminate the barbarians; under Spanish dominion the Indians
have, indeed, perished in great numbers, but

those who have survived have entered to form a constituent part of the new nation.[1]

The differing fates of the Indians under Spanish and English colonization is in part due to the rapidity of encroachment upon their territory in the one case, and the slowness of encroachment in the other case. The English have demanded that the Indian should rise almost immediately to their standard, and under this demand he is doomed to perish. The Spaniards, on the contrary, have made possible for him a gradual rise to civilization.[2]

[1] See *Democracy and Social Growth in America*, 5.

[2] In his *Travels*, Humboldt has described the process as observed in some parts of South America : "The whites advance slowly. The religious orders have founded their establishments between the domain of the colonists and the territory of the free Indians. The missions may be considered as intermediary states. They have doubtless encroached on the liberty of the natives ; but they have almost everywhere tended to the increase of the population, which is incompatible with the restless life of the independent Indians. As the missionaries advance towards the forests, and gain on the natives, the white colonists in their turn seek to invade in the opposite direction the territory of the missions. In this protracted struggle, the secular arm continually tends to withdraw the reduced Indian from the monastic hierarchy, and the missionaries are gradually superseded by vicars. The whites, and the castes of mixed blood, favored by the corregidors, establish themselves among the Indians. The missions become Spanish villages, and the natives lose even the remembrance of their natural language. Such is the progress of civilization from the coasts towards the interior."—*Travels*, i., 297.

From the standpoint of the individuals or
the tribes of the native population, the English
policy appears merciless and unwarrantably
cruel; but from the standpoint of the method
of social progress, "so careless of the single
life," if only the great end is reached, it may,
perhaps, find abundant justification.

Although the English have been more exact-
ing than the Spanish in the demands which
they have made on the aborigines of their dependent territories, although they have insisted
rigidly on the maintenance of the English
standard of civilization, they have at the same
time held their dependencies, particularly since
the fatal mistake with the thirteen American
colonies, in a much more lenient bondage than
the other European nations. In the case of
the Spanish dependency, the bonds binding it
to the mother country have been rigid and
unelastic, so that they have parted with the
first considerable strain, and the colony has
been irretrievably severed from its superior.
The English dependencies, on the contrary,
have found themselves at the end of an elastic
tie. When they have tugged to be free, the
cord has yielded, but has gradually drawn them
back when their discontent was past. Australia
and Canada may adopt a commercial policy
directly at variance with the views of England,
and still the bond of union remains unbroken.

But Spain, or the Spanish king, insisted on an essential uniformity throughout the Spanish dominions; in other words, obedience to that policy which would contribute most to the selfish interests of the mother country. The outcome of rigid adherence to Spanish policy has been the loss by Spain of her vast colonial possessions and abundant sources of wealth.

While Spain's dealing with her colonies has tended to drive them into revolt and independence, her social policy, as already suggested, has tended to preserve the aboriginal stock and mingle its blood with the blood of the immigrant population; yet at the end of any considerable period, the increase in the English colony, even when allowance has been made for different physical conditions, will be found to have far outrun the increase of the combined Spanish and native populations. This is abundantly shown by any English colonies brought into comparison with colonies of Spanish origin. Mexico and the United States do not furnish as unfair a comparison as at first might seem; for prior to 1840, Mexico, in possession of Texas and California, fairly rivalled any nation on earth. Yet during the ninety years prior to 1880, Mexico increased in population from four and one half millions to ten millions; while the population of the United States, in the same time, increased from four millions to fifty millions. The same rate of increase in these two nations, continued during the next ninety years, will give Mexico a population of twenty-four and a half millions, and the United States six hundred and twenty-five millions. Yet, in spite of this enormous increase in the United States, during the last ninety years, the inhabitants have continued to be better fed and clothed than in Mexico, and there are no indications that a lack of subsistence during the next ninety years will furnish a more efficient check on the growth of population in the larger than in the smaller nation. But whatever may be the future, the English policy, as revealed in the past, appears to be consistent with that view which, in social progress, takes account of great ultimate results rather than inferior immediate results, although the latter may be more fully in harmony with our short-sighted sympathies.

Another point of difference between Spanish and English institutions in America has reference to the affairs of the church. The contrast presented here is between the practice of toleration on the one hand, and exclusiveness and intolerance on the other. In the colonies of one nation, religion tended to become a private matter; in those of the other, it was, and tended to remain, an affair of the state. In some of the settlements of the United States, the ec-

clesiastical and political organizations were at
first merged in one, but the tendency to separate them appeared early and continued till the
divorce was complete. But in Spanish America, the alliance continued unbroken for more
than three hundred years, the church constantly gaining wealth, power, and compact-
ness of organization. It held about one half
of all the property in the colonies, and was
directed by men not always in the fullest
sympathy with those interests on which the
material prosperity of society depends. On
the economic affairs of Spanish America, as
on those of Spain, the church cast the blight
of its dead hand.

The effect of the different attitudes of the
Spanish and English colonies towards the affairs
of the church, made itself especially manifest
towards the end of the colonial period. The
fact that the settlers of the English colonies
were dissenters, bound to no strong hierarchi-
cal organization, was important, in that it rendered easy the complete separation of the
colonies from England. The Spanish colonists
were adherents of the church which had held
the unswerving devotion of the people of
Spain; thus the church of Spanish America
and the church of Spain stood as allied parts
of one great organism. When, therefore, the
struggle for Spanish-American independence

came, it was found that it was not enough to break the political bond: the bond of ecclesiastical union and sympathy remained, always drawing a large part of the several nations back to allegiance to Spain. During the struggle of the thirteen English colonies for independence, ecclesiastical alliances had little influence in upholding the allegiance of the Tories ; and when the war was ended the conflict was really over. The Tories either accepted gracefully the fact of independence, or wandered off to seek more congenial companionship. But those who upheld the Spanish rule in America, during the war for Spanish-American independence, remained, when the war was over, a powerful and dissatisfied element in the politics of the several nations. The thirteen English colonies had achieved intellectual and spiritual independence long before the war for political independence was ended; but even after the Spanish-Americans had achieved their political independence, they remained still in a strong ecclesiastical alliance with the mother country.

THE END.

INDEX.

313

21